QUIET RIOT

Q U I E T   R I O T

The Culture of Teaching and Learning in Schools

Diane Hoffman

ROWMAN & LITTLEFIELD
Lanham • Boulder • New York • London

Published by Rowman & Littlefield
A wholly owned subsidiary of
The Rowman & Littlefield Publishing Group, Inc.
4501 Forbes Boulevard, Suite 200, Lanham, Maryland 20706
www.rowman.com

Unit A, Whitacre Mews, 26-34 Stannary Street, London SE11 4AB

British Library Cataloguing in Publication Information Available

Library of Congress Cataloging-in-Publication Data

Names: Hoffman, Diane M., 1954- author.
Title: Quiet riot : the culture of teaching and learning in schools / Diane
 Hoffman.
Description: Lanham, Maryland : Rowman & Littlefield Publishers, 2015.
Identifiers: LCCN 2015036585| ISBN 9781610483094 (hardback : alk. paper)|
 ISBN 9781610483100 (paperback : alk. paper) | ISBN 9781610483117
 (electronic)
Subjects: LCSH: High school teaching—United States. | High school
 teachers—United States—Attitudes. | High school students—United
 States—Attitudes. | Education, Secondary—Aims and objectives—United
 States. | BISAC: EDUCATION / Multicultural Education. | EDUCATION /
 Comparative. | EDUCATION / Philosophy & Social Aspects. | EDUCATION
 / Students & Student Life.
Classification: LCC LB1607.5 .H637 2015 | DDC 373.1102--dc23 LC record
available at http://lccn.loc.gov/2015036585

♾™ The paper used in this publication meets the minimum requirements
of American National Standard for Information Sciences—Permanence of
Paper for Printed Library Materials, ANSI/NISO Z39.48-1992.

Printed in the United States of America

For Daniel and in memory of James

CONTENTS

PREFACE

School as we have come to understand it and practice it in the world today is probably one of the strangest of recent inventions. For much of human history, people got by very well without schools. They learned everything they needed to know in the process of engaging with people and activities in their communities.

This is no longer the case, because the ideas and practices surrounding schooling have become global norms, linked to powerful economic, social, and political agendas. Since the explosion of mass education globally in the 1950s, going to school has become a defining experience for the majority of the world's population.

Despite the importance attached to going to school, many youth in the United States never manage to graduate. Often these are bright, talented kids who can't stand the thought of another day sitting in classes, waiting for the bell to ring so they can finally get out. Or they may be kids who feel they just don't fit in. Some of them may try hard but nevertheless always end up on the dean's black list. And some may simply reject the ways school labels them as failures, even from an early age.

This is not the case in many other places around the world. While students in the United States often can't wait to get out of school, children in Haiti will walk for hours, in scorching sun and pouring rain, to spend a few hours in a school where they will sit on hard benches and be drilled in vocabulary that they hardly understand, and then they will walk home again. And they will be overjoyed to do so, day after day.

As an anthropologist who studies education, I am fascinated by the ways people learn and the impact of learning on people's lives. Most people think of anthropologists as engaged in studying remote societies, but my "remote society" is right here in my own backyard. To me, schools are settings for exploring the basic strangeness of so many of the things we do in the name of education.

When I was doing my doctoral dissertation many years ago on Iranian immigrants in American schools, I sat in a class while an Iranian student, one of the top students in the school, wrote in carefully formed block letters on the blackboard at the back of the room, "DON'T LET SCHOOL GET IN THE WAY OF YOUR EDUCATION." He was a really smart kid, smarter than he knew, because he grasped an essential truth about American education after only about a year or two in the system: Education is more than schooling, and often runs counter to it.

Schools in America today are without a doubt at the center of intense social scrutiny. Are they producing students with the skills that will be needed in the coming century, or are they failing to live up to their promise? Are they producing democratic citizens committed to the welfare of others, or a generation of selfish, entitled parents and children? Are they addressing the needs of all children, or only those of a certain race or socioeconomic background?

Since the 1990s, what professional educators call evidence-based research and practice have been widely regarded as essential to answering these questions. What this has meant is that research and reform need to be grounded in real data. There should be no more jumping on the bandwagon of innovations that look good but lack evidence of effectiveness.

There are justifiable reasons for this turn toward "what works." Key, perhaps, is that we've had a lot of stuff not work, despite often lofty goals and ambitious efforts. We desire, for example, to produce high achievement for all students, but we still have far too many dropouts. We desire to teach critical thinking, but we end up with students who can't think. We aim to teach tolerance, but we continue to wrestle with injustice and racial prejudice.

There are many reasons for these problems—hundreds of them, actu-ally—ranging from unqualified teachers, to inequitable funding, to poor parenting, to inadequate and poverty-ridden communities. In certain cases one can point to specific factors or combinations of factors that contribute to poor outcomes, but no one has quite figured out why, over the long term, intended results of educational reforms so consistently fail to be realized in practice.

This book argues that at the heart of our difficulties in schooling lies a different kind of problem from those described above. The problem is deeper and more systemic, and it lies in the culture of schools: in the ordinary ways we go about schooling, even in our most privileged com-munities.

To understand this problem, we need to go inside classrooms, where we can better appreciate the ordinary, daily activities of teachers and students. It is at this level that one can begin to see how everyday actions are patterned according to their own internal logic, often in surprising ways.

Doing this kind of inquiry requires fighting familiarity: We must chal-lenge the taken-for-granted ideas and the assumptions that often blind us to seeing the things that really matter. Everyone can look at a class-room, but not everyone can see a classroom. When we see, we realize how symbolic and how patterned things are, how much meaning lies behind even small details of what people do and say.

What we will see in the pages that follow is that, despite the sincere and often heroic efforts made by teachers to support their students, the everyday practices of schooling end up undermining the very aims they hope to achieve. This disconnect fuels a form of ordinary violence that enacts huge tolls on students and teachers alike.

In recent years, school violence has become an important area for educational research. Many things affect rates of violence, yet its con-nections to what happens in a daily basis in classrooms and the underly-ing genesis of episodes of violence in the ordinary behaviors of teachers and students are rarely explored. Instead, when dramatic episodes of violence such as school shootings occur, people talk about the need for "prevention."

I'm going to argue that if we are serious about prevention, we need to look closely at the kind of environments we create in schools. It is not about more weapons control, or less. It is not about creating "safe schools," or adding more violence prevention programs. It is not about family and community problems that spill over into schools. It is, centrally, about schools and classrooms, and the ordinary, innocent, and unconscious ways that we create a culture of ordinary violence in which our everyday actions belie our goals, values, and ideals of truth and justice.

In this book I uncover that hidden arena of ordinary life in schools, in order to generate a new consciousness about how to go about changing them in ways that can lead to greater success, and greater humanity, for everyone.

ACKNOWLEDGMENTS

Writing this book would not have been possible without the help and guidance of Rick, Jason, and many other students and staff at the high schools and elementary school I had the privilege of visiting. While they must remain anonymous, they have my deepest admiration and gratitude.

INTRODUCTION

Quiet Riot: Culture and Education in American Schools

Every day, for a good part of the year, nearly fifteen million youth head through the doors of public high schools in the United States. More than any other institution, school defines the lives of these youth, and what happens here during these critical years of personal development has lifelong impacts. While schools are hailed as places where many youth excel and are given the education they need to assume places in adult society, they can also be places where youth miss out on realizing their potential—where they experience academic failure, social exclusion, and even violence.

Both the promise and problems of schools have inspired a great deal of research. Over the past twenty years especially, studies of educational reforms have generated a good deal of quantitative data focusing on what works to improve the education that students receive. And yet, we are far from understanding many of the dynamics that continue to affect school outcomes. Despite their apparent banality, schools and classrooms are infinitely complex environments where much happens that is not readily measured or even noticed.

This book offers an interpretive, in-depth look inside classrooms in two public U.S. high schools across a thirty-year time span. Written from the perspective of an anthropologist who was privileged to shadow

two high school students as they went about their days at school, it offers snapshots of what goes on in classrooms on a daily basis. The focus
was not only on uncovering the patterns that shaped everyday talk and
behavior, but on their significance. Why did some things happen and
not others? What meanings did people give to events? How did teachers
and students make sense of things?

To anthropologists, classrooms and schools have cultures, too: They
are places where people do and say things that reflect their own position
in the world, their own sense of what is normal or natural, and their own
views of what is good and desirable. Uncovering this inner logic is what
understanding a culture is all about.

Yet the culture of classrooms is hardly ever on the agenda of contemporary discussions of what works in education. Not only has there
has been a strong trend in recent years away from qualitative research,
there is little tolerance for cultural inquiry unless it explores cultural
differences, and understanding how such differences affect school experiences and outcomes for diverse groups of students. Certainly this
is important, but there is also a need to consider the larger culture of
classrooms within which such differences exist. Every activity that goes
on in schools contributes to, and reflects, this larger culture.

This is an old idea among anthropologists of education, but one
whose time has perhaps come again. Without considering this culture,
we cannot understand the dynamics of change and reform, or the deep
roots of many of the more obvious problems that have been identified
in contemporary schools, such as bullying, school violence, academic
disengagement, or disproportionately poor achievement among certain
groups of children. All of these phenomena are connected to the often
unnoticed patterns of culture that take shape through the interaction
between teachers and students every day.

Some have called anthropology a revolutionary discipline.[1] It cul-
tivates a certain way of seeing the world that upsets the status quo,
demanding that one look beyond the accepted and taken for granted
to shed light on hidden or unacknowledged patterns of thinking and
behavior. There is something similar to the work of the psychologist in
this process, but instead of dealing with individuals, the anthropologist
focuses on groups and observations of group social processes.

Because these patterns are often very powerful but unrecognized, both the psychologist and the anthropologist find themselves more often than not in the difficult position of revealing things that may make people uncomfortable. At the same time, becoming aware of patterns of feeling, thinking, and acting that have not worked well can be very liberating, because this awareness is often the starting point for processes of change.

As a graduate student at Stanford University in the early 1980s, I was part of a research team under the direction of Professor Elliot Eisner, whose job was to go out into local high schools to shadow students. As an exercise in "Educational Connoisseurship,"[2] our goal was to describe, in rich detail, what students typically experienced every day. These observations and conversations were written up in the form of analytical essays that offered insight into the classrooms and schools we observed.

I shadowed Rick, a white, middle-class high school junior, who attended a large public high school with a diverse demographic. Rick was an average student, taking all his classes on what was called the "regular" track (that is to say, he did not take honors classes nor was he enrolled in remedial or special education). He was in the band, he did what was expected of him, and he didn't cause trouble. He was what people referred to as a "good kid."

Following Rick to all his classes and extracurricular activities for a full two weeks offered an unparalleled glimpse into the lives of students at this school. During that time the words *Quiet Riot* kept popping up everywhere—they were all over Rick's notebooks, and scribbled on chairs, desks, and hallways throughout the school. Rick explained that this was the name of a popular band. Yet "Quiet Riot" described exactly what was happening every day in every classroom. The words were a perfect metaphor for student experiences.

Captured in an essay entitled "Quiet Riot" (author, 1984), the shadowing experience later proved useful in teaching graduate student courses in research methods. Despite the effects of standards-driven reforms since the early 1980s that have been widely represented as a sea change in American education, students would always remark, with some surprise, that their own teaching experiences almost thirty years later were very similar to what was described in the early 1980s. This

raised an interesting question: What was it about schooling and classrooms that could produce such consistency, especially in the face of a
lot of different forces for change? Or was the continuity an illusion?
What had changed, in fact, from 1983 to 2009 and what had remained
the same?

With these questions in mind, I decided to go back to school in 2009
to do a restudy along the lines of the original shadowing project. A large
public high school in a relatively well-to-do community, quite similar in
size and demographic diversity to the school where the original study
had been done, served as a reasonably good comparison site. Piedmont
had an admirable reputation as one of the best schools in the state. The
principal saw the value of the project and Piedmont was interested in
learning more about students' lives.

With the assistance of teachers, he identified a student who was will-
ing to be shadowed. Jason was in his junior year, white, and taking all
his classes in the "regular," or average, academic track. He was similar
in many ways to Rick—a good kid, from a middle-class background.
Though he was not in the band, he played on the school's football team.
Going back to high school to shadow Jason would offer a new perspective on what had changed in the high school experience and what had
remained the same.

The question of change is important, if only because historians of
American education have demonstrated time and again that making true
reforms in schooling is difficult.[3] The reasons for this are unclear. While
policy changes undoubtedly have an impact on what teachers and students do, often enough the deeper structures of schooling—what could
be called the cultural practices of education—are not as readily subject to
transformation, even in the face of policy directives. Change can happen
on administrative and organizational levels, but that does not necessarily
translate well to the everyday practices one finds in classrooms.

Exploring the experiences of students deemed "average" is also
significant. The education research literature offers a good number of
studies of elite students and privileged schools, and many more studies
of blighted, urban schools, as well as studies of minority kids and minority schooling. Special education and gifted education both have large
literatures. However, there are comparatively few studies of the great
middle—those students who are not poor, not minority, not wealthy,

not gifted, not special needs. It is vitally important to explore the experiences of this group, for it is in this great invisible middle that we find the pulse—and possibly the future—of American education.

AN ANTHROPOLOGICAL LENS ON SCHOOLING

Anthropologists have traditionally considered education very broadly as the key process that underlies the existence of human cultures and societies. As the cumulative, positive change in human capacities for engagement with others and with the world, education is essential to the survival of humanity. Without education, cultures would not exist; by the same token, without culture, education, as a cultural process, would not exist.

For anthropologists, education is far more than schooling. In fact, schools as we know them today—the "egg carton" mass-market model—are rather strange places. They are neither normal nor necessary to education. For much of human history, we've managed to do without them. It is only since about the 1950s in that the world began to witness a massive expansion of formal schooling, as an accompaniment to the forces of industrialization and modernization of economies worldwide following the Second World War.

Education includes the informal kinds of learning that we all engage in every day of our lives. This includes families raising children, kids learning how to play together on playgrounds, street kids learning how to be successful on the street, or adults learning new skills. This kind of education is often described as informal because people learn without explicit instruction, without a curriculum or external measures of success, and often even without intending to learn.

Informal learning is also present in schools, and shapes the school experience very powerfully. This informal side of schooling is sometimes called the "hidden curriculum" of school. It refers to the ways schools teach a lot more than the official curriculum. They also teach cultural rules and values, and, most importantly, they teach how to be a certain kind of person who is capable of doing and thinking certain things.

Thought it may not be immediately obvious, this shaping of personhood is deeply embedded in the goals, values, practices, and policies that a school enacts. Ideally, the process produces culturally desired change in persons, whether it be in their knowledge, their skills, their capacities (mental, emotional, social, physical), or their identity. Sometimes these lessons are positive, but just as often, the lessons learned through the hidden curriculum can be negative, as classrooms are organized to produce success for some but failure for others. Most importantly, in spite of good intents and sincere efforts, the outcomes of education are not always what was intended or desired.

This hidden curriculum of schools is intimately connected to the larger political and socioeconomic environment. Schools channel these larger forces in powerful ways, even though teachers and students are often unaware of them. In combination with deeply rooted cultural understandings and values (such as choice, or individualism) and particular practices (such as academic tracking), schools actively create cultures that are both unique to their settings and representative of the larger cultural and social environments of the communities and nations where they are found. The cultural lens permits the observer to see the ways the school embodies the deepest aspirations of a society as well as its deepest fears and problems.

CHARACTERISTICS OF A CULTURAL PERSPECTIVE

To access this perspective, though, one cannot just use surveys, questionnaires, laboratory experiments, or other experience-distant forms of inquiry. Rather, understanding this culture depends on immersion in the setting so that one can appreciate what people do and think from their own points of view (what anthropologists call "accessing the emic perspective"). At the same time, it also requires keeping an analytical distance that allows one to see and understand patterns in thinking and behavior that even those who engage in them may not be aware of (the "etic perspective").

As a result, anthropologists find themselves constantly challenged to acquire both a deep familiarity with a setting alongside a capacity to see it through a cross-cultural comparative lens. The comparative lens lies at the root of the kind of defamiliarization that allows one to step back from a culture and see it against the knowledge of how things are done elsewhere. This distancing invariably sensitizes one to the fact that systems of cultural meaning and practice are not universal, and, further, that one's own practices and values are often quite extraordinary when seen against a universe of possibilities presented by other cultures around the world.

Through defamiliarization one can come to understand the cultural logic behind practices that may initially appear incomprehensible or even morally reprehensible. This is not to say that one must agree with those practices, but simply that one can step back enough from evaluating them in order to see how they can make sense and be valuable to those who engage in them.

Understanding culture also demands that one see things holistically. Though this idea includes considering things in relation to their context, it also involves connecting things across different levels of significance. What this means is that small things—the tapping of pencils, the inflection of a voice, a piece of graffiti—are "read" as if they were part of a text.[4] Small events or behaviors only have meaning because they exist in and can be read against a larger system of which they are a part. Larger meanings make it possible to understand the small things, and the small things serve as windows for interpreting meanings that exist on a much larger or systemic scale.

This is in part why anthropologists are so fond of observing in ordinary situations: They have lots of access to small things. Everyday life is an incredibly rich with things that matter even though they may appear not to matter. It is in the ordinary that anthropologists find their main texts: the patterns of meaning that are taken for granted and that constitute the local cultural logic. This logic, interestingly enough, cannot readily be articulated by those who engage in it, simply because it is so normal, natural, or unremarkable.

APPRECIATING THE STRANGE

As the eminent anthropologist Clifford Geertz pointed out years ago, one can learn to appreciate cultures that one can't commit to.[5] This kind of appreciation is very different from simply becoming knowledgeable about cultural differences or even from the celebration of diversity that is so much a part of contemporary discussions about cultural pluralism and global citizenship. Geertz rather argued that we can and should cultivate the capacity to enter into "alien turns of mind"—to immerse ourselves so deeply into other cultural worldviews that they can be experienced as equally real, valid, and valuable—things we could share, if we had not been committed to our own culture already.

It is not easy to learn cultures at this deep level. Undoubtedly experiencing other cultures will teach *something* about cultural differences, and people do learn things that challenge their assumptions in the process. However, it takes a long time—and a commitment to some pretty extreme mind-opening—to develop an ability to appreciate in a deep sense the cultural logic of a radically different way of living.

Developing such an appreciation depends on having a profound curiosity about the vast differences in the ways human beings around the world live their lives. Discovering these differences is what makes anthropologists so passionate about what they do. Often, this knowledge is valuable because it can show how ethnocentric some theories about human behavior are. It is through explorations of other cultures that anthropologists have been able to refute supposedly universal theories such as the adolescent identity crisis, the Piagetian stages of cognitive development, or Attachment Theory.

The underlying lesson is that much of what we think about the world and accept as true is often more a reflection of our own worldviews than it is an accurate representation of the rest of the world. Anthropologists strive to get beyond this imposition of their own worldviews on others, and try to accept difference for what it is. Both curiosity about differences and the demands of defamiliarization can help in this process.

Of course there is no complete escape from one's own cultural preferences and from the biases introduced from the simple fact that all human beings grow up in some cultures and not others. To combat this, anthropologists (and others who do qualitative social research) are often advised to reveal their biases in advance, to show that they are aware of how their own race, gender, and social class, for example, may affect their interpretations.

In the end, though, the value and validity of those interpretations depends on the strength of the link between evidence and interpretation: Is the interpretation warranted? Is it plausible? All social science is based on some kind of evidence and some kind of interpretation; both are always partial and subject to bias.[6] The best and perhaps only remedy for partiality is the development of knowledge and expertise in the questions at hand.

In this sense one might speak of anthropology as cultural connoisseurship: a skill of seeing that is honed and refined by long-term engagements that sensitize to qualities of human life that may not be appreciated or even recognized by others. Like a wine connoisseur or an art critic, an anthropologist offers an interpretation, based on his or her subjectivity, but grounded in evidence. To that evidence, he or she brings expertise, experience, and training in the canons of theory, in order to create a portrait that captures the logic of what it means to be a part of that culture.

There are plenty of domains in human life in which interpretations on the part of scholars and experts are accepted without making much of personal subjectivity, even though we recognize its inevitable presence. When a judge pronounces a sentence, no one expects him to accompany the decision with a carefully worded statement that he is white, male, and from inner-city Detroit. As a society, we trust that his training and expertise in the law balances out whatever influences and biases he may have as a human being. The interpretation of an art critic is also accepted, though no one demands an accounting of the critic's single-parent upbringing. Though it is impossible to engage the world without bias, there are still things to be known and learned in spite of it—and in some cases, because of it.

The main difficulty with most research-based inquiries into education is not the researcher's personal bias or background, but the conflation of normative values and preferences with so-called value-free scientific knowledge. This is evident when it comes to considering best practices in education. Many times what is "best" is quite naturally what upper middle-class parents in coastal U.S. communities do with their children. Parent-child play, extensive parent-child conversation, giving children "choices," therapeutic emotional talk: All of these things are "best," but they do not capture the value systems and cultural practices of the vast majority of the worlds' parents, let alone a good number of U.S. parents as well. Scientific evidence for styles of attachment, too, reflects keen moral evaluations that have gone unrecognized in the formation of categories for parental attachment.[7]

For anthropologists, an adequate understanding of education must include a focus on how these cultural meanings and values shape educational practices. Understanding the ways culture lies at the very core of what is said and done in the name of education is essential if we are to develop approaches to reform and change that address the deep structure of schooling in contemporary America.

THE CHAPTERS

The chapters that follow offer an interpretive, culturally based critique of classroom experiences as seen through two shadowing experiences conducted twenty-seven years apart in two high schools in California and Virginia. Though it is based on real observations of things said and done, the analysis is grounded in interpretation. There is no effort to generalize in the sense of extending the inquiry to other settings or using multiple data sites to generate themes.

That said, the interpretations offered are meant to offer insights that may be relevant to understanding the larger universe of schools in the United States. Any good interpretation goes to the heart of that which it interprets—and it is the concepts and ideas that emerge that can have relevance for explaining themes and patterns that exist beyond the settings actually observed.

Chapter 1 offers an analysis of the classroom experiences of Rick, a student at Western High School, in 1983. Drawn from the original shadowing study, vignettes offer glimpses into classrooms where daily dramas were played out. Rick's teachers were sincere, thoughtful people, who were doing their best to give students the education they thought would help them. Yet it appeared that different ends were accomplished.

Rick himself was an ambivalent player in his own education. Like most of his academically average peers, Rick merely wanted to get out of school so that he could get on with his life. Who could blame him? The larger lesson of school was that it was only the superficial, literal stuff that mattered: getting points, doing the work, and abiding by the rules. But beneath the surface of calm and order, one could read a deep malaise that was rooted in an impoverished approach to teaching and learning.

Chapter 2, "A 'Thirst' for Knowledge," considers the experiences of Jason at Piedmont High in 2009. This chapter offers vignettes from three of Jason's classrooms that capture activities, conversations, and interactions that made up Jason's days and that dramatically illustrate the ways in which students were systematically denied access to knowledge, despite obvious efforts of teachers to teach and engage students conceptually. Student "thirst" thus became a metaphor that captured more than bodily needs, but also the ways in which classrooms had become parched of genuine learning.

Chapter 3, "Paper Chase," considers in further detail the varied classes that Jason attended over a period of two weeks, and illustrates in detail the disconnections between appearances and intents and what was really accomplished, with an emphasis on the students' perspectives of classroom events. Students were acute and often accurate observers, and their comments, even when brief, reveal much about the climate of their classrooms.

Chapter 4, "Schooling Ordinary Violence," offers an analytical interpretation of what we see happening in Jason's classrooms. It suggests that the cultural contradictions experienced by both teachers and students at school constitute a form of "ordinary violence" against persons. This violence is enacted principally through a pedagogy of literalization, in which the disconnection between goals for learning and the practices meant to achieve them is present in multiple forms. In fact, I show that teachers regularly defeated their own intents and purposes.

One consequence of this pedagogy was a pervasive sense of frustration, alongside powerful evidence of student disengagement. It was not that students did not care; they were unintentionally yet systematically *prevented* from caring or engaging in any deep way with what they were supposed to be learning. Students voiced bodily as well as psychic pain as a result.

Chapter 5 is based on a comparison of Rick and Jason's experiences. Focusing on the question of continuity and change over twenty-six years, it develops a set of themes that illustrate the ways in which a deep-level cultural continuity can be said to characterize classrooms.

Chapter 6 is based on firsthand observations done in elementary classrooms. It argues that many of the patterns we see in high schools actually begin to emerge very early on in children's schooling. We can see how practices of classroom management and control become impediments to authentic teaching and learning, driving many students who want to be engaged down an early path of disengagement. We also see how teachers, sincere and dedicated, fail to connect their goals for learning with what they actually do in their classrooms.

In the final chapter, "Toward Authentic Schooling," I develop an alternative view of what it means to do authentic education. While discussions about authentic education usually advocate making school more oriented to "real-world" issues and problems, I argue that authenticity is centrally about connecting persons and learning, and that no change can really happen at a deeper level in American schooling without considering the culture of classrooms that conditions pervasive ordinary violence against persons. I also suggest eight ways that we can begin to reconsider how best to begin to change the culture of schools in ways more congruent with the goals of authentic schooling.

This book argues for a deeper look at what goes on in classrooms as key to making change. That process entails a radical questioning of foundational assumptions: about what it means to be a teacher, a student, and what it means to teach, and to learn. It means looking at schooling from a perspective that fights familiarity, familiar assumptions, familiar interpretations. It means coming to terms with what we want, and what we do in the name of what we want. This is a challenge to the educational establishment, and to all of us who are implicated, one way or another, in the routines and norms that guide it.

1

QUIET RIOT

What Is Really Done in Schools

Italian Class, Western High School, 1984:

"We are all the way to the third sentence and you don't know where we are, Jim."

"You got the place there, Lisa? What does *capisce* mean?"

Every time Mr. Mark turned his back, wads of paper shot across the room. Half the students seemed to be paying attention; the rest were passing notes to each other, staring out the windows, or combing their hair. One student handed a water pistol to another. Mr. Mark continued, "Will you come to the party? We've gone through eighteen sentences already . . ."

A student said, out loud to anyone nearby, "Why study?" Someone answered: "Yeah, good question."

Ignoring all the noise and activity, Mr. Mark pushed on: "How do you say 'shower' in Italian?"

A student replied: "*Showiamo.*" Pulling down a map, he asked, "Anyone know where Florence is? This is the language you are learning in this book." The constant chatter and activity abated only when he mentioned what would be on the upcoming test: "Under '*le montagne,*' the only thing you need to know is '*gli Alpi.*'" After going through a list of terms, he concluded, "That's all I care about that you know. I don't care about the others."

Western High was regarded as a good school. The teachers who worked there were sincere people, dedicated to their students, undoubtedly doing the best they could. Students themselves were "good kids"—for the most part they went to their classes and stayed out of trouble.

Yet in Rick's classes a majority of students appeared to be disengaged: They didn't answer questions; they left books closed; they talked, failed to do work, misbehaved, and sometimes slept. Comments heard throughout the day in almost every class pointedly questioned outright the value or purpose of school ("Why study?"). For their part, teachers clearly wanted students to be engaged and struggled to cultivate student interest, often by relating topics to current events or the supposed "real world" outside of school.

What were the roots of this disengagement? Many obvious explanations come to mind: Classes were dull or perceived as irrelevant; students were sleep-deprived, or preoccupied with social lives or other more interesting activities or jobs. All of these things were perhaps true on some level. According to some anthropologists, students naturally find schools to be alien places where resistance to classroom authority is almost guaranteed in the absence of clear intrinsic or extrinsic motivations to comply.[1] Whether or not students experience schools as caring places, too, affects their level of engagement, as students who feel teachers do not really "care" about them tend to find classrooms cold and difficult to connect to.

Most of the explanations for student disengagement point to factors either in the students themselves (lack of interest, failure to perceive purpose, fatigue, adolescent hormones "out of control") or in the larger issues outside the school—poverty, disadvantaged social status, job and family pressures, for example, that distract students from greater commitment to education. For minority students, cultural differences between home and school can have large effects.

Yet disengagement is created and negotiated in context, in each and every classroom as teachers and students interact with each other. Habitual patterns of practice and talk, imbued with meaning (or the lack thereof) constitute the currency of engagement/disengagement. This suggests that it is at the level of classrooms that a more complete analysis of student engagement should be undertaken.

THREE VIGNETTES

Vignette 1: U.S. History

Mr. David began the class with a series of handouts, as usual. It seemed that this was his way of signaling that the class had begun. He did not explain what he was handing out beforehand. As the papers were being passed back, a student said, "He likes dittoes."

Mr. David was soft-spoken and well-informed. He was also very concerned with connecting class material to current events. To this end, he brought in news magazines and played videotapes of television news programs. In fact, almost without fail, about fifteen minutes before the end of every class period he would turn on the TV.

One day, during a news show about a dead marine, Mr. David stopped the TV and tried to engage the students in a serious discussion, pointing out that this poor dead guy was in many ways just like them—the same age, an average guy, with a bright smile, and easygoing. In the middle of this, a student asked a question about Halley's Comet and the class broke into laughter. Mr. David answered patiently, as if this were nothing out of the ordinary, "We'll talk about that another time."

Rick was doodling the words *Quiet Riot* on his desk. Students were supposed to be writing answers to a quiz quietly and individually, but they were asking each other for answers and calling them out.

Later, Mr. David posed a question to the whole class, "What is the job of the secretary of state?" Rick replied, "You tell us!" After no one answered, another student said, "So, what's the answer, Mr. David?" As he began to explain, another student called out, "Jay said that already!" Kevin, a friend of Rick's, asked his friends sitting nearby, "What's he talking about?" Rick answered, "We lost him."

Mr. David reprimanded the class: "We're trying to do something so that when you walk outta here, you know a little bit more than when you walked in. . . ." His voice was serious and a little louder and clearer than normal. The students quieted down a bit.

A photographer for the school yearbook came in and asked Mr. David to smile for the photo. He forced a smile, adding, "Don't ask me to change my personality." A student crumpled up the *Newsweek* magazine that had been handed out at the beginning of class. The instant the buzzer sounded, Mr. David disappeared from the classroom. He was out even before many of the students.

One day there was a strong smell of burning in the classroom. After a few minutes, a student called out, "There's something burning!" Mr. David replied, "Don't worry about it." He continued to go over the current events sheet, as a student walked in late and sat down. He either did not notice or did not care.

A question on the sheet read, "Do you support the American invasion of Grenada?" Rick's answer was: "Yes. I think we should try to wipe out communism. I don't want to be in another situation like Iran." As the class continued to review answers, Rick called out to Mr. David, "You skipped *h*!" Another student replied, "Just go on to *j*!" Students were not following the discussion; it was difficult to hear over all the noise. Graffiti on the blackboard at the side of the room read, *Quit* [sic] *Riot*.

On the final day of the shadowing project, Mr. David appeared in class with dyed hair. The class was hysterical; Mr. David himself good-naturedly laughed with them. He began as usual with handouts, to which a student exclaimed, "Jesus! What is all this?" Jokes about his hair continued to fly, with Rick adding, "You should'a got blond stuff—you could'a been a surfer!" A student finally announced in an authoritarian voice over all the noise, "Class is in session now!" as Mr. David began speaking about Cuba.

Later, as the noise level mounted again, Mr. David yelled, "We got thirty-two people in the room. We need it quiet!" and a student called back, "Thirty-seven!" Mr. David tried to explain the partitioning of East and West Berlin, but his explanation was hopelessly drawn out and confusing. A student suggested, "Just say they cut it in half!" Another student said, "I don't understand the explanation!" Someone else said, "Shut up!" And yet another, "Control the crowd!" and finally another, "Control yourself!"

Vignette 2: Life Science

Mr. Burke was a large-bellied man with a round face; he had a friendly manner about him that made one think he was on one's side. He would yell at a student one moment, then pat him on the back the next.

Kevin said he liked Mr. Burke's way of teaching mostly because "he tells you exactly what you have to know." In fact, the notes students were supposed to take were always written on the board.

Yet on almost any day, a number of students would have their heads on their desks, sleeping. During films, which were very frequent, this number would increase to about half the class. Mr. Burke never made any effort to awaken those who were sleeping. He simply ignored them.

Mr. Burke usually reacted strongly to misbehavior and rowdiness as soon as it interfered with his teaching. "I'll give you five or six detentions. If you wanna fool around, do it on your own time." "Shut up! I tell you to shut up, do you hear?" Once, when he was trying to answer a student's question, the class got too noisy and he asked, "Hey, should I answer this question or not?" A student called back, "No! Don't answer it!" The noise level of this class was consistently high, except during films—when people slept.

There were some instances, however, when students expressed genuine interest; this usually happened when Mr. Burke provided real-life illustrations of a concept. For example, during a discussion about blood types, he talked about difficulties in getting rare blood and about blood donations. Students asked how much a pint of blood costs and about the experience of giving blood. But as soon as the discussion returned to the textbook, the entire front row resumed staring out the window.

One day Mr. Burke started class with instructions to copy down what was written on the board. A student walked in late and took his notebook out of a side cabinet; papers fell out. After a few reprimands about the noise level, Mr. Burke told students to begin working on problems. Some students were still not clear as to what the assignment was and were asking each other. At one point I heard him tell someone, "You'd better learn something so you can get a good job and get rich."

Vignette 3: English

"Ladies and gentlemen," Mrs. Hubbard began, handing back a series of graded quizzes, "John is reading . . . Mary is reading . . . Steve is not reading . . . Tom is not reading. . . ." She was a small woman with intense blue eyes and a constantly changing expression. Her style was dramatic; she modulated her voice and gestures as if she were onstage.

Notebooks were open here; it was quiet as Mrs. Hubbard performed. "Ladies and gentlemen, please get out vocabulary list number eight. Lisa, vocabulary list number eight. Quiet." Her voice was soft, each word clearly enunciated. She used individual student names constantly, either to pose questions, reprimand, make requests, or praise.

Despite the fact that the class was reading a novel at the time, two days were spent going over the same list of twenty vocabulary words. Vocabulary did have a number of advantages: It was concrete, tested easily, and presumably could be memorized. But one student, Kevin, said the book they were reading was too easy for him; he read it in two nights.

During the second week of shadowing, Mrs. Hubbard introduced a Poe short story, telling the class they would see a film based on the story rather than read it because the "vocabulary is too difficult." The students were also given instruction in writing during the second week. A simple mechanical model of what an essay should look like was provided, with rules such as: "The thesis statement is always the last statement of the introduction." Students were given no leeway in elaborating or not following these rules. Points would be taken off if everything was not exactly where it should be.

Over the course of two weeks, Mrs. Hubbard discussed themes in the literary works twice: one ten-minute discussion for the novel and one five-minute discussion for the Poe short story. During these discussions, she asked leading questions, prompting "right answers." If a student came up with something original in response or tried to express a deeply felt opinion, she said something like, "That's a good idea," but then passed on to the next question or to another student, leaving the "good idea" behind.

Once a female student began her response to a question with a tone of frustration in her voice, saying, "What I'm trying to say is that. . . ." Her idea was complex, but Mrs. Hubbard immediately dismissed the comment and brought the discussion back to a simpler level. In another instance during the novel discussion, a student made a point and Mrs. Hubbard exclaimed, "How interesting!" and then moved on.

Her "Reward the Reader" quizzes would have been better called "Reward the Teacher" quizzes because that was the real function they served, and students seemed to know this. Once, in a show of resistance perhaps, many students turned in blank answer sheets. When they were corrected (papers exchanged and graded by other students) and Mrs. Hubbard realized that few students had answered, she told them, "Shabby performance."

In this class, earning points and getting answers were what counted. Being tardy and cutting resulted in grades being lowered. A student asked, "How much does a cut take off?" Mrs. Hubbard replied, "Two-thirds of a grade." Student: "Can we bargain?" The answer was "No." Mrs. Hubbard handed out an exercise sheet with questions based on the Poe story. Then she turned on the taped reading and said, "You'll get all the answers right now."

On the last shadowing day, Mrs. Hubbard showed a movie version of *Dr. Heidegger's Experiment*. After the film, she began a discussion about some of the ideas in the story and students got fairly involved in talking about the message of the author. But after a few minutes, Mrs. Hubbard ended the discussion sarcastically: "I can see that was a profound experience for all of you." She dismissed the real interest the students had expressed, undermining her own efforts to create engagement. With that deflating comment, she defeated the very enthusiasm she so wished they would have.

MAKING AND UNMAKING STUDENT ENGAGEMENT: THE PARADOXES OF PRACTICE

These vignettes reveal students and teachers engaged in a peculiar struggle: While on one level teachers obviously want to foster connection and engagement, and students clearly show at some points that they are capable of such connection, this intent seems to be ineffectual at best, or even dramatically undermined. One could explain this by saying that the difficulty lay in individual idiosyncrasies—Mr. David's soft-spoken demeanor, for example, that allowed and even encouraged students to rebel in spite of everything he did to the contrary to engage them; or Mrs. Hubbard's dramatic performance style that emphasized show, perhaps, over real substance; or Mr. Burke's no-nonsense style of just telling people what they needed to know.

Yet to do so would not really get at the dynamics of practice that in effect were similar across all four cases. What teachers actually said and did in classrooms was shaped by their participation in a larger conceptual environment that reflected a pervasive accounting orientation. In this accounting, knowledge that "counted" (literally, in terms of points or grades) was pitted against knowledge that "didn't count."

Teachers actively participated in this process by regularly telling students what knowledge counted and what didn't, thus dismissing a good part of their own teaching as irrelevant. Mr. Mark even said more than once that he did not care if students did not learn most of what he talked about as long as they knew the things that were going to be on the test. It was only the things that were going to be graded that were important: They were, quite literally, the things that counted.

In doing so they also undermined whatever inherent interest the material might have had. Students were exposed to this culture throughout the school day at Western. In even the best classes, there was no valuing of any subject matter material other than what contribution it could make to the student's credit/point accumulation. Opportunities for expression of genuine interest in subject matter were consistently cut short or even undermined, leading in some cases to genuine frustration on the part of students.

Another aspect of this literalization was the primacy given to "just the facts" or to discrete elements of categorical knowledge. Except for Mr. David's history class, there was little conceptual-level discussion or explanation in any of the classes. Instead, there were lists of vocabulary words, rules for writing paragraphs, rules for calculating genetic inheritance, names and places, verb conjugations, adjective endings. Students would be told, "Put this under 'x' in your notes," or "This is what you have to know to write your essay," or "Know all the facts relating to blood types." Even when students were clearly interested in conceptual and thematic analysis, as in Mrs. Hubbard's class, they were repeatedly silenced.

Further, while valuing engagement with classroom material and wanting students to achieve, teachers had clear limits on what they believed students could achieve or, perhaps, wanted to achieve. They thus demanded little beyond the most basic cognitive tasks, even when students occasionally struggled to assert that they wanted to and could do more. One of Rick's friends, Steve, criticized teachers as "going too slow" or even as incompetent. He was incredulous that his English teacher couldn't spell "Los Angeles." He said he was failing a math class he could readily pass because it was too easy. For him, "School looks like a zoo, doesn't it . . . ? I could teach any class here."

Contrary to what teachers thought, it was not because things were too difficult that students failed; it was because things were too easy. As a result, they disengaged. In a sense, both students *and* teachers disengaged, even though they both continued to go through the actions of teaching and learning so that the culture of accounting could be maintained. For teachers, the disengagement was manifest in the ways in which they undermined their own efforts; for students, it was manifest in the rumbling of the "quiet riot" that could be seen and heard everywhere.

A RETROSPECTIVE: WHY DON'T TEACHERS DO WHAT THEY SAY THEY WILL DO?

Perhaps about fifty years ago there was a time when anthropologists were very concerned with what they saw as a basic educational problem: Why was it so difficult for teachers and schools to accomplish their goals? If teachers said they wanted students to be engaged learners, why were they systematically doing things that could only produce disengaged learners? If they valued diversity, why were they devaluing it in practice? As formulated by George Spindler, the idea was that American education seems to suffer from a fundamental disconnect between its intents and its outcomes, or between its ideals and what is actually practiced in schools and classrooms.[2] This idea echoed throughout the writing of a generation of anthropologists and sociologists of education writing through the 1970s and into the 1980s.

Spindler's iconic analysis of the teacher Roger Harker (1959) is perhaps the best-known example of this problem. Roger Harker was a white, middle-class teacher, well-respected by his peers and dedicated to his students. He sincerely believed that he treated all his students equally in the classroom, priding himself on being fair and just with all children.

But rigorous observation of his classroom proved otherwise. In fact, his interactions with the children showed a clear bias toward those who were most like himself: white, middle-class, successful, go-getter types. He was not giving children equal chances to participate, in spite of his self-professed goals and his own self-perceptions. He defeated his own aims and was not aware in the least that he was doing so.

Spindler was clear, though, that the problem wasn't with this individual teacher or with this particular school per se. It was a problem in the larger culture of which schools were a part. Schools and teachers were agents of a system engaged in cultural transmission; they transmitted not only elements of cultural heritage, but also the conflicts that were inherent in the culture itself. If the larger culture had problems connecting its goals with its practices, then schools would, too.[3]

The most important reason for focusing on this failure of intent was the role education was supposed to play in building a democratic society. While we hailed ideals of equality, access, and democracy, for example, the ordinary institutional practices of schools undermined these. Teachers and participants in the system thought they were doing a good job, though, and seemed to be unaware of the discrepancies between their goals and practices.

Other anthropologists who considered this problem also emphasized that teachers as individuals were not to blame. For example, Eleanor Leacock wrote in her analysis of New York City elementary schools that it was the "failure of present educational practices" that led "well-meaning and hard-working teachers to mis-educate children."[4] Teachers were sincere actors within a system that was culturally structured to mis-educate.

At the middle of the twentieth century, many prominent anthropologists of education developed this critique. They focused on revealing the inner workings of mainstream educational practice and the ways in which it variously failed to live up to its promises.[5] They had a program of social amelioration in mind—"visions of a better world"—in which anthropologists could offer insights into present practices as well as alternatives to them.

The French-born anthropologist Jules Henry, for example, wrote powerful critiques of the culture of schooling in America. He painted dramatic portraits of how teachers inadvertently undermined their goals and created learning environments that were mere shadows of what they intended. For Henry, there were systems of sham in place that supported not seeing outcomes that conflicted with cherished self-perceptions and convictions.

It was not only a question of schools or classrooms, however. Practices of child-rearing also suffered from similar discrepancies. Writing in the 1960s, for example, the anthropologist Solon Kimball critiqued the new movement toward "child-centered" education as a delusion. He saw it as a way for adults to believe they were raising a more natural, healthier, freer, better-adjusted child, while they were really putting ever greater pressures on the child by overdirecting the child's activities and constantly making sure that they taught the child important social and cognitive "skills."[6]

In another case, Valerie Polakow's (1992) comparisons of five day-care centers illustrated how in all schools but one, actual practices were in clear conflict with espoused ideology and intent of the school and its teachers. Of the five centers observed, only one—the African American center—in fact had any degree of conformity between its stated objectives and its actual practices. Similarly, Robin Leavitt (1994), in her research on day care, showed how institutional practices in fact undermined the espoused ethic of caring for children.

In sum, what Spindler, Henry, Leacock, Polakow, and others described were cultures of educational practice systematically blind to their own outcomes, and in fact organized to defeat their own purposes. It was not just that there were hidden messages behind educational activities that were unintended, or that people could operate with different and even conflicting interpretations of events. Rather, it was a deeper problem: One could observe people throughout the culture whose actions systematically contradicted their own beliefs and values, though they never realized it.

EDUCATION AS CULTURAL TRANSMISSION, AND BEYOND

How could this be? How could educators be so blind to their own practices? Anthropologists' concern with discrepancies in educational goals and outcomes was derived from a basic understanding of education as a process of cultural transmission. On the one hand, there were values, aims, purposes, and meanings that formed the heart of culture and that needed to be inculcated in the next generation. Schools were key settings for this process. On the other, it seemed that the mechanisms or procedures that were in place to support this transmission were faulty. The idea was that if we could only focus on better alignment between activities and goals, problems would be solved.

Today, the theory that drives thinking about education is less about breakdowns in transmission and more about education as a *cultural practice*, in which ends and means are less easily separated. Practices themselves embody actors' ideas and values at the same time as they embody the cultural and structural meaning systems in which they are located. The idea is that if we stop trying to get inside of people's heads, and stop thinking of education as a problem of translating theories into practice, we may better focus on how practices embody dynamics of theories, intents, goals, and meanings as they interact with the constraints imposed by organizations and institutions.

Jean Lave is an anthropologist who has done extensive work on exploring how people learn in ordinary activities and settings outside of classrooms and schools. She calls this process "situated learning," and she sees it as deeply connected to social life, social interactions with others, and the development of personal identities. Learning itself is embedded in practical activity, not separate from it. When people try to abstract teaching and learning from the situations in which they are found, they engage in decontextualization, with negative consequences.

According to Lave, this happens fairly often in classroom teaching. Precisely when teachers think they are doing good things for students by specifying the components of an activity precisely, or breaking it down into pieces that are clear and self-contained, they generate a literalness of meaning that, in fact, changes what can be learned from the situation. They end up actually creating more ambiguity in the process, and ". . . shrivel[ing] the meaning of learning for all concerned."[7]

This is perhaps why the students at Western had such trouble with apparently simple tasks, such as vocabulary worksheets. Instead of giving students opportunities to think deeply about concepts, teachers thought they were doing them a favor by making things simple, stripping them of their complexity, or specifying things precisely. But these efforts undermined the concepts—the real heart of what was to be learned. With nothing to learn, students naturally responded by disengaging and going through the motions. Their disengagement was a rational response to the kind of "learning" demanded of them.

REWORKING AN ANTHROPOLOGICAL CRITIQUE OF SCHOOLING

Anthropologists' concern with discrepancies in educational goals and outcomes was grounded in a conviction of the fundamentally purposive nature of education as an activity to improve the capacities for human engagement with the world. This concern is not less significant today and is arguably more significant than it ever was, given current global conditions that are creating new forms of inequality in schooling and generating new tensions over how best to prepare children and youth for the future.

What this demands is a new sense of what it means to do critical scholarship on education that is more inclusive of the importance of looking deeply at practices. Obviously the larger social structural contexts remain significant because these constrain practices in important ways and can introduce huge social disparities and inequalities. Much critical research and theory in education has focused on the ways these larger inequalities structure the outcomes of schooling in fundamentally inequitable ways.

Useful as it is, critical research has neglected the experiences of average students, who don't fall into the categories of obvious social disadvantage or racial or ethnic difference. Nor does it really address the dynamics of everyday classroom practices as they are experienced by students. With its underlying focus on the ways differences in social advantage and inequality play out in schooling, it has prevented a different use of the word *critical*: one that might consider the failure of good intentions via the ordinary dynamics of classroom interactions.

What Rick's classroom experiences at Western reveal is not so much a problem of poor teaching, although obviously there were many things that teachers did (such as start a class with handouts) that could be criticized. The larger pattern of school as Rick experienced it was shaped by a paradoxical culture in which the failure of good intentions was played out through ordinary practices. Engagement was a good intention but practiced in ways that undermined it. Valued on the surface, learning was devalued in practice—reduced to facts and figures, piecemeal knowledge that became the currency for points and credits. In a sense, from a student's perspective, the simpler things got, the more difficult they became.

The contradictions between what people intended and wanted out of school and what they ended up accomplishing were not the fault of teachers or anyone in particular. What an anthropological eye draws us toward is a consideration of the larger culture that makes such problems possible and even, perhaps, simply unremarkable. It takes looking at student experiences to make sense of them.

2

A "THIRST" FOR KNOWLEDGE

Algebra Class, Piedmont High, 2009:

Carol, a student in Coach Stump's algebra class, was sitting at her desk holding her hands to her head like it was going to explode. Suddenly she slid from her seat and collapsed on the floor, screaming, "Too much pressure!" The whole class jumped up and crowded around her. Coach Stump left the room to go find the school nurse. As she lay writhing on the floor, the assistant teacher asked her, "What did you eat?" Another student raised his hand and circled his index finger, giving the military "move out" signal. Everyone filed out into the hallway. Carol was still on the floor screaming.

Coach Stump returned and told everyone to gather in the school's central outdoor courtyard. Sitting on a picnic table, he resumed addressing the class. "What we need to do is finish what we started. I'll give you a few more minutes to finish up. Stay within this general area. . . . We'll go back in ten minutes and get this checked." One student lay on the grass, sunning himself. Some emergency personnel carried Carol out on an orange stretcher.

A student turned to me and said, "You're doing research on what high school's like again? It's, like, painful!"

ORDINARY VIOLENCE AND SCHOOLS

Piedmont High was very unlike the image of a typical violence-prone inner city school. It did not have metal detectors, scanners, numerous security cameras, or a major police presence. According to Jason, there were "a lot of fights," but the atmosphere in general was calm, orderly, and pleasant.

The usual view of violence in schools focuses attention on physical assaults, shootings, bullying, and other forms of overt and covert physical or emotional aggression. Though helpful in some ways, this view tends to highlight violent acts apart from their larger context. Anthropologists have argued that violence should rather be seen as "folded into the ordinary.[1]" It is present in the ordinary acts of everyday talk and behavior that deny individual capacity, dignity, or rights. The roots of this ordinary violence are located in society at large, particularly in the imbalances of power and social inequalities that exist. Cultural and social practices, while appearing unexceptional or "normal," may also contribute to ordinary violence, masking its cumulative or damaging effects.

Bodies, too, reflect those processes of social structural violence. Their physical symptoms speak to the conditions of life that individuals face. Often the illnesses of the body, whose proximate causes may be explained using reductive, biomedical explanations, can never be fully understood without also seeing how they express an individual's experiences in culture and society. Illness is the body's symbolic language; the body rebels, rejects, and suffers in particular ways that are symbolic of individual experiences of social tensions or injustices. Carol's "too much pressure!" can thus be read on another level: the body itself speaking out against the larger social context or culture of what was happening at the school and perhaps beyond, as well.

Ordinary violence exists in many institutions, and it can be found in schools, too. However, this is not just because schools exert control, or silence the voices of students and teachers. These phenomena are important and have been discussed at length by others. And it is also not just because they channel the effects of larger social structural inequalities, such as poverty and racial discrimination, into real effects on students' lives. All of these things are true, as well. There is another source of ordinary violence that has yet to be fully explored, and it is connected to the life of classrooms themselves: to the ways teachers taught, their interactions with students, and the larger systems of meaning that shaped these. Exploring what daily life was like at Piedmont leads to another level of understanding of the dynamics of ordinary violence as it emerges in schools.

PHYSICS: THREE VIGNETTES

First Day

"Okay, what we're gonna do today—a lot of people out!!!—is not much new material. So many people out—it must be the water, better watch out! . . . Kiddos, we're gonna learn about electrical power today and do some practice exercises. You're gonna have a test on Friday. What will be on the test? Okay, the pages in the book that the test will be on are thirty-five to sixty. I will give you familiar problems in this format [she draws circles illustrating Ohm's Law using V/I/R]. You're gonna need this law."

A student sitting at the back of the room, Jeremy, asked under his breath, "Do we actually have to know something about physics for the test?" All the students had their backpacks, still zipped up, lying on their desks. Only Jason actually had a notebook out. Ms. S. reminded them that there would be a visitor in May who would talk to them about magnetism. Jeremy asked, "Is he gonna be upset if we talk out of turn?"

"Okay, what we're going to be doing today won't be on the test. Where is Zach?"

Jason replied, "Skipping, like normal."

"Remember when we studied energy? Now we're gonna study power." Ms. S. began writing on an overhead projector. "What's energy measured in?"

Jeremy: Jules.
Ms. S.: No, what did I tell you. . . .
Jeremy: Watts.
Ms. S.: Watts is short for. . . .
Jeremy: Wattage. Hey, those are my initials!
Ms. S.: How do I find electrical energy? Energy = qV [on overhead]

Jason, alone among the students in the class, was taking notes. Another student had his head on his desk, arm stretched out holding a water bottle.

> Ms. S.: You don't need to know this for the test!
> A student: Do we have a test Wednesday?
> Ms. S.: Oh, for the love of God, what are we doing on Wednesday? A movie!

She continued writing on the overhead: P = IV V = IR . . . "Is that pretty clear? Let's look at the packet. I'll go through sample problems five and six."

> Jeremy: Are we doing anything fun?
> Ms. S.: Yes, this is fun! On Friday we're going to look at appliances.

She worked through a problem, and then said, "Now, this will not be on the test." She repeated the statement three times.

Jeremy asked, "Is that gonna be on the test?"

A black student was asleep with his head on the desk.

Ms. S. continued, "Okay, now do one on your own. Look at all the happy faces!"

Jeremy asked which problems they should do. As the students began to work, comments began to flow. Nick said, "You're killing me. You're killing me!" Another student announced, "I'm tired!" Ms. S. replied, "Period one was even more tired than you! They were real good, that's why I gave them a break."

Nick asked, "When are we gonna have a party in here?"

"We'll do it toward the end of the year, cuz most of you are seniors. . . . Come on, kiddos, I'm not making you do too many! Come on, Jeremy, wake up, do it! This is easy!"

A student asked, "How am I supposed to do this problem?"

Ms. S. replied, "Was I speaking Russian when I explained this?"

> Jason: On number thirteen, do we have to do C?
> Ms. S.: No, just A and B.
> Another student: Can I get some water?

Ms. S.: Didn't you just get water? Come on, boys. . . . Malcolm, did you write this down? Come on, Malcolm. . . . You're up next. In question A, what variable are you looking for?

Jason and Jeremy started to talk about a recent dance, and Ms. S. said, "Jeremy! What are you looking for?"

Jeremy: I don't know. . . . The answer?
Ms. S.: We just did a problem like this!

Another student had his head on his desk and was flipping a pen.

Ms. S.: Make sure you have the worksheet. Remember I gave you an outline? We're almost at the finish line! Just make sure you have all the stuff you need to study.
Jeremy: Are we studying?
Ms. S.: There will be conceptual questions!

Somebody else asked for permission to get water.

Ms. S.: Are you guys dehydrated or something?
Nick: I'm just tired.
Ms. S.: This is the last time you'll see me before the test.
Jeremy: Do they pay you a lot to teach us?
Ms. S.: You guys can't afford me. . . . Did you guys ever figure out that you torture each other?

As students began talking among themselves, Jason called out, "Two minutes!"

Jeremy: This is depressing.
Another student: I'm gonna sleep in my next class.

Another Day

"Zach! We missed you," said Ms. S. as he entered the room. She reminded students about the upcoming test and told them explicitly about the format of the problems that would be on the test, even showing an example on the overhead projector. "You don't need to know kilowatt hours for the test, but we're going to start doing that today." A student asked about something else being on the test and she said it would not; he replied, "Thank God." Another student added, "Oh my God, yes, it's like torture."

As they went over homework problems, Ms. S. said, "Number twenty-five is the type of problem that will be on the test. It's important to know this. . . .Wake up, boys! Jason! [Jason had his head on his desk.] . . . Number thirty-six! You need to know this for the test! . . .Okay, I'm gonna give you one more sheet of practice problems."

A student: I thought we're supposed to do the lab and stuff . . .
Another student: I'm tired . . .
Ms. S.: I'm tired, too . . .
Student: Do you have a pencil?
Cam: Can we use our notes?
Ms. S.: Just do your work!

She threw a pencil to the student. Zach was tapping on his desk; Wilson was pushing a tissue through a hole in a cup.

Ms. S.: Come on there, Zach . . . Stop staring into space.

Cam asked a question, then got up and handed his paper to Ms. S., who said, "You already did all of these?" A cell phone rang. Noticing mistakes in Cam's work, Ms. S. said, "One is not the answer . . . It makes me nervous when you don't know these variables. It's unacceptable . . . Number one is wrong, number four is still wrong. . . ."

Zach started flipping his calculator cover up and down. Cam asked to leave the classroom to get some water.

"Here's an idea, Cam. Get water BEFORE you come to class . . . I'm stuck in here without water . . ."

Cam: I'm just thirsty . . .
Ms. S.: Let's settle and drop the water topic. Okay, number one. A toaster is rated one thousand watts. That's POWER. A lot of people didn't know that's power. What letter represents current?

Cam: *R!*
Ms. S.: No, that's resistance . . .

Cam was spinning his calculator. It dropped on the floor.
Jason was fiddling with a set of keys in his backpack.
Wilson pounded his desk and put his head down.
Jason said to someone, "Isn't that a water bottle?"
"Wilson, what's twelve hundred watts? So, we're looking for *I*, right?"
Wilson was tapping his pen. Jason looked back at the clock and yawned.

Ms. S., catching this, said, "Jason! What does *I* represent?" Jason gave a correct answer, and Ms. S. said, "Excellent! Cam, did you get this one?"
Cam replied, "No . . ."
"Okay, the cost of electricity is not going to be on the test."
She handed out worksheets. Cam leaned back in his chair with the sheet balanced over his face.

"Okay, watts is a measurement of power. Kilo means a thousand. So, a kilowatt is a thousand watts. So, how would you convert watts in kilo-watts? You divide by a thousand." She wrote on the overhead projector: *p=100W=.1kw.*

Wilson shook his head violently. Students were tapping pens, and after a few minutes Wilson put his head down on his desk.

"Guys, write this down! You're not very good with unit conversions—we did this at the beginning of the year!" She went through a number of conversions on the overhead, such as converting seconds into hours, minutes into hours, etc. After this she said, "I want you to figure out how many kilowatts each of these appliances uses. That's all you have to do today. All your power usage should be in kilowatts. Does everyone understand what we're doing?"

Wilson got up and grabbed another tissue from the class tissue box with a flourish. Students got up to read the labels on the various appliances in the room.

Ms. S.: What's power measured in?
Some students reply: Watts.

She directed the students to look for a number with a W next to it.
Cam said, "This is trifling."

Ms. S. replied, "It is trifling. . . . It's vexing and trifling at the same time. All the power in kilowatts and all the time in hours!"

A string of questions from students followed: "Where are the amps?" "So, how do I convert thirty-five minutes into hours?" "How many hours are there in a day?"

It was almost time for the class to end. Ms. S. asked the students to hand the worksheets back to her "so you don't lose them."

Wilson zipped up his backpack and blew his nose loudly.

Yet Another Day

"Okay, guys, take out your homework. I know you're chomping at the bit. . . ." A student pounded his desk in reply. "You actually have work to do. It's called physics. Does anybody know what happened to Zach?"

A student replied, "He's gone to live on the streets."

"Okay, who did their homework? I know Jason did it. . . ."

Jason was fiddling with a lock and key.

"Those of you who didn't do it, what we're gonna do is go over kilowatt hours and the cost of electricity." A student put his head down on the desk as she talked. "So, I'm gonna go over that activity, because next week you will have a quiz on calculating the cost of electricity. . . ."

Jason asked, "So, what do we have to know?"

Ms. S. continued explaining the material and interjected a comment about people not being able to afford the cost of electricity, with "the young and elderly most at risk."

At one point, she said, "What would you do without me teaching you?" A student mumbled something under his breath, and she replied, "I heard that. . . ."

Someone else said, "This is just the same stuff over and over again. . . ." The student who mumbled earlier got up and put something in the trash can.

Using the overhead projector, Ms. S. began to explain how to calculate the cost of electricity, but she soon interrupted herself to ask, "Malcolm, is there a reason you're not writing any of this down?" She continued, "You have to find the power in watts. What do you have to do?"

Malcolm answered with a loud yawn. He still did not write anything down. As she went through a similar problem yet again, she said, "It's the same thing over and over again."

Ms. S. continued going over practice problems for the next few minutes, asking students for answers. Wilson offered an answer, "I got sixteen watts," but he was rubbing his eyes as he did so, and Ms. S. asked, "You all right? I hope you're not crying cuz you got that wrong. . . ." A few moments later, as they discussed the next problem, Wilson again shook his head violently.

Jeremy took a huge pile of disorganized papers out of his backpack, then put them back, having retrieved two plastic tubes with the words GOURMET SCENTED_____ on them.

"Here's the grand finale, Wilson! You ready? Folks, did you get this?"

Brian offered an answer, and Ms. S. asked, "Does everybody agree?"

Jeremy said, "Sounds good."

Ms. S. kept asking, "What'd you get—somebody! Wilson? Malcolm? Wilson's my superstar today!" Wilson finally answered.

Ms. S. said, in disbelief, "Hello?"

Jeremy replied, "Lucy, I'm home."

Jason got up to use the hole punch.

Ms. S. continued, "So now what we're gonna do—I'm gonna give you a sheet. Now, some of you may still have it. You remember I gave you a packet that had power problems on it." She held it up. Jason was still at the hole punch. She said, "You okay there, Jason? Technical difficulties?"

There was some grumbling about the sheet, and she said, "Come on, boys, you can do it. It's not that hard." She assigned just two problems for them to do. Jeremy asked, "Just fourteen and fifteen?"

"Yes, just those two problems." Another student asked which problems again.

As they were working, Wilson said, with exasperation, "I don't know how to do this!"

Ms. S. replied, "You DO know how to do it! We just did it!" At this point, someone's phone rang. "Whose phone is that?" The ringing stopped.

Jeremy was talking to Justin, who was sitting next to him. Ms. S. addressed them, "I doubt you're doing physics."

Justin said, "I'm trying to learn!"

Ms. S. replied, "I'm trying to teach!"

She walked over to him to offer some help, asking, "Were you here when I showed you this method? Come on, Justin, focus!"

She looked over at Jason, who had his hand on his head, and asked, "What's wrong, Jason? Your brain hurts?"

Jason replied, "Yes! I'm confused!" She went over to him to explain again how to solve the problems.

Jeremy asked, "Do you think you can just tell me the answer to see if it's right?"

"I'm gonna go over it. I want to remind you I won't see you tomorrow. Are we done?"

Wilson leaned back in his seat.

"Number fourteen! Number fourteen! Justin? First thing, what's the power? What'd you get?"

Jeremy answered, "10.8."

"10.8 kilowatt hours. . . . Did you get this, Wilson?"

Wilson said he didn't do it.

"Well, do it right now!" She turned to Jeremy. "Do you want to do another one or are you good to go?" Jeremy said, "Good to go."

"Since most of you haven't done the homework, you can have ten minutes to do it."

Jeremy started to work, but others had already started to pack up their things.

A "THIRST" FOR KNOWLEDGE

Ms. S. was a sincere teacher who genuinely liked her students and made what some might even call heroic efforts to teach them. She explained clearly what would be covered on tests and what would not be, she gave students heads-up warnings about upcoming tests and quizzes, and she explained schedules for class activities. She went through problem after problem illustrating the correct procedures for solving them. She attempted to engage students' interests with films, guest speakers, and hands-on activities.

Yet something was going wrong. For the most part, students appeared to be minimally engaged, if at all. They put their heads on their desks, asked for permission to leave the room, slept, fidgeted. Some might say that this was a class of mostly seniors (Jason, though, and a few others were juniors) who had already "checked out" of school, or who were more interested in parties and their personal lives than their education, or who were suffering from adolescent hormones that made them incapable of engaging with classwork.

But to do so would be to once again avoid looking at what is actually going on in classrooms. It was not that students weren't interested or had no desire to learn or that they couldn't learn. They were clearly intelligent; in fact, they showed vibrant interest in some of the discussions that Ms. S. initiated with regard to everyday issues such as the cost of electricity. Even more tellingly, they expressed critiques of what was happening, aware that what they were being offered in the name of learning was something of a farce. As Jeremy pointedly asked at one point, "Do we actually have to know anything about physics for the test?" Cam called the material "trifling," and another said, "This is the same stuff over and over again!"

Indeed, most of each class was spent on going over the same kinds of problems repeatedly, emphasizing definitions, terms, and procedures. Ms. S. did this because students seemed not to know how to solve them. Both teacher and students were frustrated. "How am I supposed to do this problem?" said one, and Ms. S. replied, "Was I speaking Russian when I explained this?" When she asked, "What are you looking for?" Jeremy said, "I don't know . . . the answer?" Then Ms. S. said, "We just did a problem like this!"

The difficulty was that endless procedural drill, where problems were approached mechanically, was never going to help. What was missing were the concepts that lay at the heart of the subject matter. In this endless apparent simplification, students were actually reduced to asking, "How many hours are in a day?" and converting hours into minutes. They were being "dumbed down" by an approach to teaching that missed the conceptual heart of what they were supposedly learning.

Though Ms. S. believed she was teaching "concepts," she was substituting procedural and mechanical tasks for conceptual-level thinking.

She did this to help students—but what she did not see was that her best efforts to break things down, to go step by step, to stick to a very mechanical approach to solving problems, defeated her own goals of engaging them at all, let alone at a conceptual level. It was, in sum, inauthentic teaching.

Students themselves perceived this and shut down. Jeremy said a number of things that revealed his understanding of the situation—most of which were either under his breath or ignored by the teacher. "Do we actually have to know something about physics for the test?" he asked. At another time, Ms. S. asked him, "Jeremy! What are we looking for?" and Jeremy replied, "I don't know . . . the answer?" Later, in a testimony to the extent to which students did not appreciate the endless step-by-step, break-it-down approach, Jeremy said, "Do you think you can just tell me the answer to see if it's right?" Once, when Ms. S. held up an electric blow-dryer, she read the words, *Electrocution if dropped in tub.* Zach replied, "So we shouldn't drop it in the tub?" He was parodying the literalness of the exchanges that regularly happened in this class.

It is in this context that student "thirst" was symbolically significant. Students repeatedly asked for permission to leave the classroom to get water, saying they were thirsty; Ms. S. even noticed, as she said at one point, "Are you guys dehydrated or something?" She started out a lesson one day by saying, "It must be the water." Water bottles were objects of attention. A veritable battle over water happened in nearly every class.

But again, as in Carol's unfortunate event, the body was speaking. Student thirst was an embodied metaphor for their experiences of a classroom that was devoid of any genuine learning or knowledge. They were thirsty for an authentic learning that they were systematically denied. Students' thirst for water was a critique of what was, in effect, the conceptual desert of the classroom. Water was a symbol of the life that was being denied to them, to everyone. More than simply a bodily need, it was a telling metaphorical riff on the parched intellectual and emotional climate of the classroom and the school.

Thirst, moreover, existed alongside plentiful expressions of pain and suffering. Nick said, "You're killing me. You're killing me!" Another said, "Oh my god, yes, it's like torture!" Students repeatedly said they were "tired," and Wilson would shake his head violently from time to time; even Ms. S. said, "You guys torture each other." Jason had his hand on his head, saying his brain hurt; he was "confused."

The manifest disengagement of students in the class, alongside embodied metaphors of thirst and pain, could be seen as an entirely rational and unexceptional response to a pedagogy that was in many respects a form of ordinary violence. It denied students' capacities to engage at higher levels with the subject matter, impoverishing and locking them in, as it were, to a kind of dead-end farce, a mere imitation of "learning."

For sure Ms. S. did not intend this; in fact, her intent was quite clearly the opposite. She did all she could to make things easy and accessible for the students, trying mightily to connect them to the subject. And there is nothing necessarily wrong with learning procedures; they are often essential. But this approach eliminated the very thing students were so thirsty for—genuine conceptual engagement that would allow them to "make sense" of procedures and hence to learn in an authentic way.

It would be easy to dismiss Ms. S. as simply being a poor teacher; yet to do so would be to overlook the larger culture in which she taught and the fact that what happened in her classroom was not unique. In fact, many of the same things happened in Rick's classrooms twenty-seven years earlier. We see the same emphasis on procedural teaching at the expense of conceptual engagement, the same sorts of self-defeating pedagogy (often painting students as not wanting to learn or not interested). We also see sincere teachers who are trying to do a good job but not quite conscious of how their intents are mistranslated in practice.

This contradiction between intent and what actually happens in classroom teaching is central to the way ordinary violence functioned in Jason's classrooms. It may sound extreme to consider this a form of violence, yet if we consider the discourse of students at school and the extent to which metaphors of pain and suffering were ever present, it begins to make a little more sense. Carol's pain was real; as was that of Wilson, with his violent head-shaking, and Jason, whose head hurt. Thirst, too, was a form of suffering.

Yet these embodied metaphors escaped the teachers; they were unheard messages. When Carol collapsed during the math class, the teacher simply moved the class outdoors and continued with the lesson, as if nothing had happened. By not engaging with the students at these most critical moments, teachers inadvertently contributed to the alienation students were already feeling. The student who chose the word *painful* to describe what high school was like captured an essential truth.

3

PAPER CHASE

You always have homework.
High School teachers are treating you like adults.

—Sign on wall in classroom

Piedmont High, German class, 2009:

German class was held in a trailer behind the main school building. Mrs. P. sat on a chair in the center of a rough circle of about eighteen students. There were a couple of phrases in English ("we play tennis") written on the board, and students were translating them into German. As they finished, they brought their papers up to the teacher, who checked them. "Zuper!" she said, handing one back. She chatted amiably with the students in German, going around the room and asking everyone where they were from.

The trailer room was jam-packed with stuff: paper snowflakes hung from the ceiling, a giant purple monkey wearing a hard hat sat atop a huge filing cabinet, along with a couple of teddy bears; empty book boxes and stacks of papers were piled all over the floor; there were miscellaneous desks, tables, a TV in the corner, and cabinets filled with more books and papers. The walls were covered with decorative paper plates, posters, collages, and signs. There were about twelve large boxes of Hammermill printing paper stacked up at the side of the room that read, "99.99% jam-free."

When the translation exercise was finished, there was another in which students wrote their names on papers and then exchanged the papers with others, at the end of which they handed all the papers back to the teacher. A student went up to the teacher to have a permission slip signed and left.

"Okay, zuper, y'all!" Jason opened up his notebook to a new blank page. Many students were without notebooks, though; they just stretched back in their chairs, arms crossed. Mrs. P. explained something at the board, then tossed a pile of papers on the floor. Students came up to pick them up from the floor, and then they exchanged those papers with each other.

At the end of the period, Mrs. P. gathered a pile of green papers from the floor under her chair and handed them out. These were "self-evaluations." As students exited the room, they handed their papers back to the teacher, and a girl asked if she could have extra points because, she said, "I helped pass out papers."

INTENTS VERSUS REALITIES

German class was a veritable paper chase, as handing out papers, filling out papers, reading papers, exchanging papers, throwing papers on the floor, and picking them up again mediated almost every classroom activity. Not only were activities centered on managing paper, but paper was literally everywhere: covering the floor, the walls, and even hanging from the ceiling in the form of paper plates and snowflakes. The student above, who asked for extra points because she "helped pass out papers," recognized that passing out papers was as valuable as, say, writing an essay. Perhaps the most eloquent symbolism was the twelve boxes of Hammermill printing paper stacked up in the room that read, "99.99% jam-free." The irony of this was that students and teachers were buried in so much paper that rather than make teaching and learning "jam-free," it choked them to death.

Obviously, the teacher did not intend for this to happen. Paper was supposed to facilitate teaching and learning. Instead, the circulation of paper became the primary raison d'être for the class. This was not the only class in which paper was important. In Jason's other classes, teachers often started by either handing out papers or asking students to take out papers or notebooks. While intended by teachers as signals to engage, paper was effectively a signal to disengage, as completing worksheets took precedence and even replaced face-to-face teacher-student interactions. Often students failed to even carry their notebooks, refused to open them, or left them open on desks while doing nothing. Not a few of the notebooks (particularly among boys—Jason's included) were so jam-packed with papers in such disarray they seemed virtually useless for anything besides storing more papers.

Paper, like water, was imbued with meaning and significance. In Jason's classes it was a principal indicator of "doing school," providing some reassurance perhaps to teachers and students alike that they were engaged in schoolwork. At the same time, just like student thirst, it represented a pedagogy that was drained of life.

Algebra, Day I

Algebra was taught by the school's football coach, Mr. Stump, who worked with an assistant teacher. As class began, the phone rang. Mr. Stump answered, and as he talked, he directed the class, "Get your 'Do Now' sheets out and get to work on that."

The students were working on factoring equations. After they finished the "Do Now" exercise, they went over some homework problems, and then took a quiz. There was a constant rattling noise coming from somewhere, possibly an air vent.

Coach Stump went over a problem. He had a small square with four compartments drawn, each with a factor. "Now, what's the first thing we do? What are we factoring? . . . The next step is to look at the top row. What do they have in common? They have an x." He crossed out the x, saying, "You got to pull it out. If you don't it'll mess up your table. Now we're gonna work on creating a multiplication table. $19x$ times what gives you $19x$?"

A student replied, "One."

"Good. When you pull them out of the box, look above the box and to the side of the box."

He did another problem using the same technique. "What's our first step gonna be? What always goes in the top box?" It was a purely mechanical approach; there was no explanation at all of underlying concepts. Ironically, though, on the next problem, Mr. Stump began by saying, "Okay, now it's the same *concept*. . . ." He again drew a box, put the factors in the boxes, saying, ". . . remember, the variables of the middle terms always go in these boxes. . . ." As he talked, the air vent continued to rattle loudly, and a girl started drumming. A student was asleep, head on his desk. Mr. Stump went over and tapped him on the shoulder to wake him up.

It was now time for a second quiz. "Please clear everything off your desks." The assistant teacher handed out the quiz sheets, saying to a girl, "Do you understand what we're doing?" She shook her head no. Another girl said, to loud laughter, "What period is this?" The assistant took the girl outside the room, either to provide extra help or, more likely, as a disciplinary measure.

As students finished their quizzes, some read, others started whispering to friends, and others slept. Jason noticed a friend asleep on her desk and he reached over to her. She raised her head and pounded the desk loudly. While waiting for students to finish, Mr. Stump sat at his desk, flipping his pen.

After the quiz, he announced, "What we're gonna do now is a discovery activity with perfect squares." He handed out sheets of paper. "All you gotta do is find the square root. . . . There are two columns of numbers, one for squares and another for square roots." During this exercise a single boy answered all of the teacher's questions; no one else talked at all. It was like a dialogue between the two of them. As this went on, there was more tapping on the desks. A student was tapping on his calculator. A couple of students turned to glance at the clock on the back wall. Mr. Stump reminded them of the homework: "Just page 68 for homework. Just six problems. So not a whole lot of homework." The bell had not yet rung, but there were already two students at the door.

Algebra, Another Day

The coach began by saying, "All right, guys, get your stuff out." Someone had written on the blackboard up front behind him, "I think this class rocks! NOT." He handed out sheets of paper drawn with large boxes. On the smartboard was a "Do Now" exercise: *Factor the quadratic: 3x. . . .* He reminded students there would be a test on Friday. After a few minutes he went over the problem: "What did you get? How many did not get that?" Nobody answered. He then handed out another sheet. Jason put his empty "Do Now" sheet into his backpack.

"We got four terms now instead of three, so this may get a little complicated. What goes in the box here?" The same student who always answered the teacher's questions replied, "Four." Coach Stump said, "You don't have to think to find any of these numbers." A girl then asked, "So it doesn't matter what you put in each one?"

"Let's do number two. Let's put *A* over here." He went through the same mechanical process. "Okay, now you do numbers three to twelve on your own." He went around the class to offer help to individual students as they worked. "You need to pull out as much as you can pull out!" After a bit he returned to desk at the front and sat flipping his pen.

A student said, "I don't get it!"

A cheerleader at the back of the class was eating a large red candy apple. Another girl took out a Snickers bar. The smell of hand lotion wafted over the class.

A while later, they reviewed the answers. The same student who always answered Coach Stump's questions volunteered an answer to the first one, then Coach wrote the answers to the others on the smartboard.

"Do your sheets!" he reminded them.

ARE WE LEARNING ANYTHING?

Worksheets, exercise sheets, and question sheets played a prominent role in Coach Stump's class, as they did in many others. But it was also clear that students were not taking much away from doing them, if anything, nor were they understanding the "explanations" for problems they were being given. Students repeatedly said they did not "get it" or didn't understand. It was not that they did not care about learning; it was that they could not learn. They voiced their criticism of the ways they were being taught in subtle but unmistakable ways, as in the comment of the girl who asked, "What period is this?" or sometimes more blatantly, as in the comment written on the board: "I think this class rocks! NOT."

They could not learn because there was nothing to learn; that is to say, the approach to teaching was lacking. There were, in fact, no explanations and no concepts—the heart of what could have helped students to "make sense" of what they were doing. Instead, they were asked to fill out boxes, again and again. In lieu of any sort of genuine connection with the subject, students did anything they could to make the period bearable, from eating to personal grooming. And sometimes, too, they just collapsed.

What was worse was that the teacher thought he was teaching "concepts," even calling one activity a "discovery" activity, even though there was nothing to discover. At some deep level, the teacher himself had confused teaching concepts with mechanical or procedural methods for solving problems. Indeed, as Coach himself said, "You don't have to think to find any of these answers," inspiring one student to reply, with point-on irony, "So it doesn't matter what you put?"

If thinking was not required, what was there to engage with? Would plugging away at filling out boxes ever really teach anything? The students were being given a shadow activity in the guise of "mathematics." There was nothing for students to learn. Students were caught in the contradiction between what the teacher thought he was doing and what he was really doing.

This contradiction formed the silent backdrop for teaching at Piedmont, and it took many forms. But in each case, students were denied access to deeper conceptual engagement with subject matter. They were, in fact, being denied the only thing that really mattered. Their education was in many ways a sham.

American History

As Mr. Roberts's teaching assistant described an upcoming group poster activity, a black girl was sucking on a lollipop at the back of the class; after a bit she began drumming on the desk. After a few more instructions, the teaching assistant said, "I'm gonna go around and check your papers."

A boy wearing a hunting cap said out loud, to no one in particular, "We don't learn nothing. . . ."

Mr. R. addressed the class in a booming voice as he proceeded to go through the day's material.

Mr. R.: Secession is when states decide . . .
Students call out: To leave!
Mr. R.: So they leave. What states stay?
Jason: Missouri.
Mr. R.: Missouri. What else?
Student: Tennessee.
Student: Missouri.
Mr. R.: We got Missouri . . . How about Maryland?
Student: Baltimore . . .

Another student sighed audibly.

Mr. R.: What do you know about West Virginia?
Student: Coal!
Student: Mountains!

Another student began whistling.

Mr. R.: Why was it so important to keep Virginia?
Student: DC!
Mr. R.: DC, okay . . . [If not] what are you gonna have to do?
Student: Move the capital.
Mr. R.: Why do we need to keep Kentucky?

The other student was still whistling.

Mr. R.: What do you know about riverbanks?
Student: Slippery!
Mr. R.: On the SOL test they're gonna ask you about the Deep South, the border states, battles. . . . We did Fort Sumter. The next battle is. . . .
Student: Antietam!

Mr. R.: Where was the Battle of Antietam?
Student: Maryland.
Mr. R.: Any other battles we're doing today?
Student: Appomattox.

The black girl with the lollipop had slid low in her seat, almost hidden behind the backpack on her desk.

Mr. R.: Have you got the border states stuff down?

Jason was tapping out a rhythm on his desk.

Mr. R.: Lincoln issues the . . .
Students: Emancipation Proclamation.
Mr. R.: What's gonna be gone?
Students: Slavery.
Mr. R.: I'm gonna ask you the same question on the test.
Students: Okay!
Mr. R.: What officially ended slavery?
Student: How many years did that go on?
Mr. R.: What do you want me to explain?
Student: [answers . . . inaudible]
Mr. R.: They got to keep their swords and . . .
Students: Horses!
Mr. R.: General Lee encourages the soldiers to go home and be good
    . . .
Students: Citizens!
Mr. R.: You guys know where Arlington is?
Students: Yes!
Mr. R.: There's only one thing we left out.
Student: [saracastic] What did we leave out?
Mr. R.: This was a war created by whom? Fill out your sheets!

As they filled out the sheets, some students copied answers off of other students' sheets. After they were done, Mr. R. said, "I was gonna show a Civil War film with you, but . . . "

Student: Let's just chill!
Mr. R.: Okay.

It was almost dismissal time. Class was over a while ago. The three black girls at the back of the room had their heads on their desks. There was a poster on the wall of James Dean in *Rebel Without a Cause*. (Students were actually watching the film in Jason's English class.) As the end neared, students began crowding at the doorway, ready to bolt at the sound of the buzzer.

History, Another Day

After some preliminaries, Mr. R. resumed his signature "fill in the blank" style of instruction.

Mr. R.: All of those things are the result of what revolution?
Jason: Industrial.
Mr. R.: How do you fight?
Another student: Defensively.
Mr. R.: Once you sign up, you're in the army till it's . . .
Students and Mr. R. himself: OVER.
Mr. R.: Did they have any way to track the people?
Student: No.
Mr. R.: Grant will have to send some . . .
Student: Troops.
Mr. R.: Lincoln is the president who allows who to vote?

At this point he began a film on the Civil War, but he kept stopping it every few minutes to ask questions and provide comments.

Mr. R.: That's really the only way you had to . . .
Students: Remember things!
Mr. R.: But we developed new technology . . .
Students: Cameras!
Mr. R.: How do these things make you . . .
Students: FEEL?

All three black students in the class were sleeping with their heads on their desks. Jordan, another student, also had his head down. But Mr. R., apparently content with letting the girls sleep, gave Jordan no such grace.

Mr. R. boomed, "JORDAN!"

Jordan woke up. Mr. R. showed another thirty seconds of the film before stopping it again, saying, "Karl Marx! He wrote about a form of government called. . . . "

Students: Communism!

He started the film again. After thirty seconds he stopped it again to show the place where the Battle of Chancellorsville took place.

Another student had his head on his desk. Jordan got up to get a pink slip from the class TA and left the room.

Mr. R. started and stopped the film again, saying, "That's Daisy. Daisy was the daughter of a . . . " This time he provided his own answer: ". . . soldier."

The narrator of the film said, "The greatest battle ever fought was about shoes. . . . "

Mr. R. stopped the film again and said, "No, that's a lie. It was about roads . . . If you want to fight, you must find . . . "

Students: Roads.

After a few more starts and stops, with more "fill in the blank" type questions, it was almost time for dismissal. The three black girls were still sleeping. The teaching assistant was also at the back of the room, but she did nothing to wake them. At 3:30 the film was still on, but students were glancing back at the clock.

Mr. R. was a sincere, dedicated teacher who wanted his students to do well on the state standards of learning examination. His approach to teaching—the "fill in the blank" technique—could be explained in that light. It did engage students in face-to-face exchanges, and it was probably a better way to make sure the necessary "facts" were covered than simply having them read passages from a textbook. At the same time, however, it, too, diminished students' engagement with the subject matter by reducing it to a mere fill-in-the-blank activity.

So in important ways students were being denied access to deeper themes and concepts that would promote authentic learning. The student who said "we don't learn nothing. . . ." at the beginning of class one day had it right. Though many people believe the major problem with schools is that students "don't care," that interpretation does an injustice to students. Quite the contrary—students were exquisitely sensitive to and critical of the ways classroom teaching was failing them.

As Jason said one day, "It's really hard to drink water during the day at school." He said this while reflecting on Carol's collapse in math class, adding that he believed it was due to "lack of water." He continued, "Maybe when the new principal comes, they'll put in a new bunch of rules. . . . Lately there's been a lot of fights. And we need to cut down on the eighth period crap. The school's overzealous. We should get a freedom-of-speech wall like the one downtown. . . . Right now I just wanna get outta here. The main reason to come to school? It's socializing. I want to see my friends. It's to have fun is the main way I think of it."

The second reason is that for Jason, getting a high school diploma represented money in terms of a future career: "Every hour I'm here. . . . It's a thousand more dollars. . . . I could get a better education at home—my mom is a genius—but my friends are at school. Some teachers are just like lifeguards—they just babysit the kids, [but] special education teachers come in handy—special ed teachers will come in and get you out of class."

If anything, Jason believed they needed to shorten the school day and school year, because, he said, he was "bored four or five hours a day." He liked the block scheduling, because he understood that they were trying to "make school feel like college," but ". . . they should break it up. Break it up so it's not like so much pure misery. . . . School's almost like a prison now. They've got one lady, her whole job is to figure out who skipped what period. If they find out you skipped, it's like, 'Your son is going to become a male stripper in Vegas! Good luck!' I've seen her office. It's like this top-secret place with all these spreadsheets and charts."

Interviewer: "It seems they treat you like little kids here."
Jason: "They treat us like INMATES! . . . They say they treat us like adults, but it's like a communistic country. . . ."

Study Hall

About half of the students appeared to be working on school tasks; the others were listening to iPods, sleeping, reading newspapers, filing nails, combing hair, or chatting with friends. The teacher went over to wake a sleeping student.

Suddenly everyone jumped out of their seats and crowded near the windows that faced the breezeway. A girl had collapsed on the ground. Jason and the teacher left the room to go get help. As they did so a black girl called out, "Okay, everybody, back to work!" A police officer arrived to help the girl outside.

When Jason returned, he said it was probably a seizure. The teacher came in a few moments later and announced, "Okay, everybody, back to work!"

4

SCHOOLING ORDINARY VIOLENCE
Rebel Without a Cause

"Even if you don't want the fries, they give them to you anyway."

"Bells are so constant here you don't even need to hear them."

"We don't learn nothing . . ."

"My philosophy is, you can win the battles, but you can't win the war . . ."

"I think this class rocks . . . NOT."

"You're doing research on what high school's like again? It's like, painful!"

There was a rebellion going on at Piedmont, but no one recognized it. For the most part, it was a quiet rebellion, manifest in currents of unrest, movement, sarcasm, disengagement. Students voiced criticisms, and even more powerfully, perhaps, their bodies were talking, through metaphors of suffering, pain, and collapse. Teachers and students found themselves locked into patterns of classroom life that were essentially contradictory. It was a contradiction between the goals and ideals that the school aspired to (e.g., "Teachers are treating you like adults") and the realities of everyday educational practice ("They treat us like *inmates!*"—in the words of Jason).

This contradiction took various forms, but it permeated nearly every interaction between students and teachers. It created a school culture organized around deception, as people were unable to recognize the ways their efforts to achieve certain outcomes were defeated by the practices they engaged in. Or, even if they recognized the fissures, they could not voice them or act on them. This was a culture of ordinary violence, because it prevented participants from achieving the learning and humanity they were capable of. As a consequence, quite naturally, both teachers and students responded with exhaustion, frustration, resentment, disengagement, or, more dramatically, collapse.

The girl who said "let's get back to work" voiced a fundamental critique of the school's inhumanity: its failure to recognize the experiences of students and to provide space for discussion and possibly for change. In both cases of collapse, teachers ignored the situation and simply pushed on, without so much as an acknowledgment that something dramatic had indeed taken place. Or was it that student collapse was not dramatic at all? Perhaps it was so normal, so unremarkable, as to not even merit any mention. In either case, the "back to work" ethos normalized student suffering, casting a veil of silence over what was inordinately visible. In so doing, it highlighted yet another contradiction: What is seen cannot be said, at the same time as what is said cannot be seen.

THREE VIGNETTES

Vignette 1: Study Hall

There was a veritable musical chairs going on as students and teachers came and went throughout the period. There were two teachers in the room. It was quiet. The two black girls whose desks were next to each other were not in class, though their books were open on their desks. A black boy (the "exec") was seated at a desk covered with newspapers, set apart from the others at the side of the room; he got up and left. Another student, Eli, left the room. Then another girl who was sitting near Jason left. One of the teachers left, too. Then the two black girls returned. Eli returned. The exec returned to his desk. Jason went to the computer terminals that were lined up at the front of the room. The two black girls were talking.

A girl had her head on her desk, doing nothing. The exec was chilling. Another black girl also had her head on her desk, while doing a worksheet. The two black females continued to talk.

Eli left. Jason left. One of the teachers left. Another black boy left. Jason returned. Another girl left. The black boy returned. The remaining teacher chided a boy for not working. He got up to get a newspaper from the exec. A black girl was combing her hair. The teacher started patrolling the class and told the black girls to stop talking. Eli came back. Jason was listening to his iPod and writing a letter to his girlfriend. The second teacher came back. Students began packing up.

Vignette 2: Algebra

"I need to check your review packets. The rest of the time is your own."

This seemed to be a cue for students to start coming and going. As soon as Coach said this, two students entered the room and two left. The student who always had the answers got up to borrow a calculator from Jason and then left, too. There were twelve students in the room at 12:50; about five had the worksheet review packet on their desks, but even fewer were actually working on it. A student asked her friend, "Did you finish this?" and she replied, "No, I lost it." Instead, she was working on what looked like a journal for an early childhood education course.

At 1:05 there were five adults in the room: Coach Stump, his teaching assistant, plus another math teacher, Jason's study hall teacher, and finally another gray-haired teacher or aide. Not only were students moving in and out, teachers were moving in and out, too. They were not conferring with each other, and other than Coach Stump and his teaching assistant, they were not involved in teaching; they were just there, undoubtedly taking care of some personal business. Coach Stump sat at his desk while his teaching assistant stood up front to explain a problem.

Carol had her head on her desk; a boy nearby had a worksheet in front of him with his calculator out, but he was not working at all. Two athletes at the back of the room talked and joked continuously. Another student nearby was doodling. The three "extra" teachers left. Carol finally took out her review pack and got up to borrow a calculator.

Coach Stump then said, "All right. I'm gonna do a review session on factoring with this box." He drew a box on the board, and proceeded to go over the mechanics of filling out the box—the same stuff they'd been working on for almost two weeks. The doodling student had drawn an angel-like figure. The girl was still working on her early childhood assignment.

A student came into the room with a calculator. After getting up to use the stapler, Carol tossed the review/practice packet on the floor next to her backpack, sat down at her desk, and put her head down. Jason tried to toss a wad of paper into the trash can from his seat, missed, and went to pick it up. Carol was now using the calculator, but after a few moments she slammed it on the empty desk next to her and rubbed her eyes. The assistant teacher gave her a sharp look from across the room and said something to her about sending her out of the class; she then said, angrily, "I'm not gonna annoy you if I haven't done anything! What did I do?" Nevertheless she picked up her backpack and left the room. Another adult visitor entered the room.

Coach Stump said, "All right, we're going to do GCS factoring! A little mini-review. All right, come on. . . ." Students went up to him individually for help or explanation of the procedure, but class ended in the middle of this activity.

Vignette 3: English

"Let's all take out our papers and books. . . . Hopefully you've finished the book. You should be able to answer the questions on the board. . . . If you haven't finished the book, don't write this yet. Read chapter twenty-five. I'm gonna give you till lunch to do this. Any questions? Okay."

There was silence. A student dropped a book on the floor with a loud *thump*. The teacher sat at the front of the class behind a laptop. A girl had a notebook on her desk, closed, that said BLUE DAY on the cover. She was not doing anything. A while later, Mr. T. looked up from behind his laptop and, seeing the girl just sitting there, mouthed something to her. She began to read the novel.

About twenty minutes into class, almost all the students were reading. A black male student looked up from the book and yawned. At 11:05, most were still reading; three were writing. The black student left the room. A female student got up, walked to the trash can, and spat out a wad of gum, shoving a backback on the floor with her foot on her way back to her seat. The teacher was still buried in his laptop. There was a loud bell, signaling time to go to lunch.

When students returned to class after lunch, Mr. T. engaged them in a discussion about the book they were reading, *Catcher in the Rye.* He asked individual students, "Mr. A., what do you have to say? Why does he go on the carousel? What's the other interesting thing about the carousel? Think about chapter two earlier. What does he tell Phoebe he wants to be when he grows up? A catcher in the rye. He catches the kids before they fall off the cliff. Obviously there's some sort of symbolism there. . . ."

A student said, "This is depressing." Mr. T. replied, "Why is it depressing? What effect does this have on others?"

A female student got up to deposit the remains of her lunch in the trash can.

Then there was another loud bell—this time, an announcement: "Teachers, please excuse the interruption! Would you please read your e-mail from Ms. Allen at this time?"

After a brief exchange with the TA, the teacher returned to the book discussion. "Why does he tell P. to shut up?"

A girl said, "You don't tell your best friend to 'shut up.'"

Mr. T. continued without acknowledging the remark. "If you compare the last chapter and the first chapter. . . . It's one of those limited happy endings. Did everybody get that? That he's telling the story from a mental hospital?" He read a relevant passage. "You'll see this in *Heart of Darkness* next year. . . ."

A student: Do we have to read that? It sounds boring.
Mr. T.: Any other interesting observations?
Another student: It's kind of like. . . [inaudible].
Mr. T.: What does that mean?
Student: I don't know. . . . Okay, I get it, it's kind of like a flashback or something.
Jason: He's also saying, throughout this whole book, if you don't have connections, if you don't need others, then everyone is isolated. They are all isolated from each other.

Mr. T. nodded, but he did not address Jason's idea.

A discussion followed on other topics for a few minutes, and Mr. T. concluded it with an announcement that he was changing the due date of the essay to May 5. He continued, "Last class we did some free writing; the next step is to come up with an introductory paragraph with a thesis sentence. Really make sure you do this, because you don't want to fall behind. Open your literature text to page 399." The page in question was headed "Literary Interpretation: At a Glance." A box highlighted the elements: *Clearly identify the author. Give a statement of the theme. Present evidence (quotes). Take into account other interpretations.* Mr. T. said, "That's all you need to do for now, write that introductory paragraph." A couple of questions followed about the mechanics, then the students closed their books as the teacher began to show the James Dean film again—*Rebel Without a Cause*—asking, "Now, where did we leave off?" The film continued until the bell rang. Students used this time to exit the class with a variety of passes.

AN INAUTHENTIC PEDAGOGY

The disconnect between said ideals and the actual practices seen in classrooms was evident, first of all, in classroom pedagogy. In nearly every class, the teaching was mechanical or procedural. The logic was that breaking things down into steps or offering literal, mechanical strategies that "don't require thinking" would make things easier for students. But that was exactly the problem: Students could not follow easily. In fact, this teaching, which teachers considered to be "conceptual," was anything but. Without concepts, there can be no learning, as there is nothing to help the pieces or procedures hold together and make sense. This absence of conceptual-level teaching constituted a fundamentally inauthentic pedagogy. It promised, but did not deliver. And in so doing, it created enormous frustration for teachers and students alike.

Substituting the Tangible for the Intangible

This inauthentic pedagogy took varying forms. In some cases, as in Jason's German class, it involved substituting the tangible for an intangible; ie., paper—in all its forms—became the essence of learning. It was no longer a *means* to instruction, but the very raison d'être of instruction. Paper was also symbolic: Like the lack of water, paper represented a kind of "dehydrated" instruction: form without substance. Worksheets abounded in most of Jason's classes; student notebooks were invariably packed with papers, and completing them was taken as evidence of engagement and learning. In fact, they had little to do with learning. In this sense they were empty signifiers, as Jason himself inadvertently revealed, stuffing an empty "DO NOW" exercise sheet into his backpack.

Confusing the Concept with the Procedure

Confusing the concept with the procedure was another aspect of this contradiction between intent and practice. Teachers *wanted* students to have a conceptual grasp of their subject matter; they wanted students to be engaged in a deep way. To that end, they thought they were doing students a favor by breaking everything down into basic steps or sequences of procedures, or rote-style "fill in the blank" exercises. In practice, however, this literal approach to instruction only made things more confusing and less inviting for students. In the case of Coach Stump and his factoring boxes, students went through problem after problem in an entirely procedural way: "What goes in the top box?" etc. Students did *not* understand what they were doing (as they clearly said at various points); there was no connection ever drawn between filling out the boxes and the conceptual meanings involved in factoring. Yet the teacher talked about the "concept" and even gave students what he called a "discovery activity"—using the same procedures.

In Jason's history class, Mr. Roberts's signature "interrogation" style consisted of whole class fill-in-the-blank statements, all period long, every single day. Students dutifully stepped up to supply the words to complete his sentences. Though there was never any discussion, there were some occasional comments by the teacher that indicated he did have an interesting and critical perspective that he could have shared with the students (e.g., when he pointed out that the film's claim that the war was fought over shoes was wrong, that it was about roads). But even at that point, he fell back into the fill-in-the-blank trap, effectively silencing the possibility of any deeper engagement. Yet he wanted to students to appreciate the material at a deep level, and he was committed to students doing well on their exams. He had a great knowledge of and appreciation for the subject he taught.

The only discussion of any conceptual depth witnessed during two weeks of observations occurred in Jason's English class, when the teacher tried to engage students in talking about the book they were reading. But even here, there were plenty of missed opportunities. When students brought up interesting or valid points that reflected their own thinking, they were sometimes ignored, as were student criticisms (e.g., "Do we have to read that? It sounds boring . . ." to which the teacher replied, "Any other interesting observations?"). Jason himself offered up a very good comment that the teacher merely recognized with a nod, instead of building upon it. On one occasion, during a discussion, a student was told, "You went beyond what I was even looking for!" but, as this comment revealed, expectations that students could and would be engaged at a deep conceptual level with the class material were minimal.

Teaching for Self-Defeat

The pedagogy of self-defeat refers to the ways teachers themselves undermined their own goals to get students to be engaged and to learn, by minimizing the work they asked students to do, emphasizing how little they were asking of students, or explicitly teaching material but then dismissing its value by telling students they "don't have to know it" for the test. Why should students pay attention, then? Why exert any effort when it's not going to matter? Nearly all of Jason's teachers tended to make comments such as "Only six problems! That's all I'm giving you for homework," or other comments that emphasized how little teachers were asking of students. Sarcasm was prominent among some teachers, such as Mrs. S., who regularly said things that clearly indicated she did not expect students to be engaged or excited about the material.

Teachers also signaled their own disengagement through powerful body language. Many times they would assign a task and then basically "check out" of the class, as did Mr. T, Jason's English teacher, who used to sit up front buried behind his laptop for most of his classes while students (supposedly) read or wrote paragraphs (according to the "rules" for writing paragraphs). Or, like students, teachers would exit the classroom, assign students some seatwork, and then retreat to their desk to catch up on work, or sit flipping pens (as did Coach Stump).

Allowing students to sleep or otherwise tune out of the class was another way teachers reflected their acceptance of defeat. Teachers tolerated all manner of student behaviors, including sleeping, placing heads on desks, grooming (hair combing, applying hand lotions), and snacking—some of it quite obvious, such as the girls who sucked on lollipops in history or the one who sat at the back of Jason's math class eating a large red candy apple while the teacher was addressing the class. When teachers bothered to wake sleeping students (which was not often), it was always the white students, never the blacks. It seemed they had already given up entirely on the black students.

SURVIVAL STRATEGIES: MOBILE BODIES

In every class, students were almost always coming and going; sometimes the same student would come and go multiple times during a class period. Giving passes to exit classes was rampant. If students could get out of a class, it seemed, they did. This was especially true during study halls, where half or more of the class might be missing at any given time.

In some classes, even teachers themselves migrated in and out: Aides, special education teachers, assistant teachers, and classroom teachers themselves often left classes for periods of time. In study halls, where no instruction was going on, this was perhaps to be expected. Yet this was true in other classes, as well.

Student and teacher circulation in and out of classes revealed another important contradiction. Though teachers stressed the importance of focus—often using that very word—the actual practice within classrooms, with its constant inflow and outflow of bodies, made focus virtually impossible. Obviously, there were reasons: Teachers and students had personal business to take care of and they didn't have any other time to do it. The school lacked classroom space, which meant that in some cases teachers had to share a classroom. There were also teaching aides and special education staff who visited classrooms. Yet movement shaped practice in ways that undermined any possibility of coherence, continuity, or focus in the learning experience. It was a case in which the school, as an institution, was in fact unintentionally organized to defeat its purposes.

From the students' perspective, it seemed the major unofficial reason for students to be constantly circulating in and out of classrooms was to escape boredom, pressure, and confinement. Since actually cutting classes had become a cause for severe disciplinary action, students did the next best thing—they circulated in and out. Jason implied as much when he said that special education teachers were useful because "they can get you out of class." In a telling reflection on the extent to which students needed to escape, a few minutes before the end of nearly every class students would gather at the door, ready to bolt the instant the bell granted a merciful release.

Meanwhile, throughout the day, in every class, one could sense an undercurrent of noise and ceaseless movement. If students were not sleeping, they were tapping, drumming, dropping stuff loudly on the floor, slamming books or calculators on desks, sucking on lollipops, whistling, getting out of their seats to get tissues, throw stuff in trash cans, use staplers—anything just to move! The only class where this behavior was not evident was in Jason's weight-lifting class. There, students were *supposed* to move. They engaged fully, and moved freely from activity to activity. This was, not surprisingly, Jason's favorite class.

One of the more bizarre phenomena that appeared in Jason's classes was the "first responder." In English, math, and physics, there was one student who usually dominated the interaction with the teacher, including answering most or in some cases all of the teacher's questions (in English it was Jason himself). Whatever the responder's personal reasons were for taking on that role, the end result was that the rest of the class could maintain their state of relative disengagement, while the teacher's focus was directed to the individual responder. If there was just one student who bothered to answer the teacher's questions and appear engaged, then the rest of the class was off the hook, so to speak.

What were the roots of student disengagement? It originated in the lack of authentic teaching. Without authentic teaching that effectively practiced what it preached, there was nothing for students to learn. Every subject was stripped of its conceptual life and made shallow, or empty. No wonder students were not engaged: There was really nothing to engage with.

Classroom pedagogy itself was thus a source of ordinary violence: Students were told to learn, wanted to learn, but then they were not given anything to learn. How could one not be frustrated? There was a class at Piedmont for students considered to be at-risk. It was called "Jump Start." The parallel to a dead battery was clear. But it wasn't the students who were dead. It was the education they were receiving.

PAIN AND DEFEAT: THE DEHUMANIZATION EXPERIENCE THROUGH STUDENT EYES

It is tempting to offer a reading that paints these classrooms as a classic case of teachers and administrators exerting excess surveillance and control, and students suffering the consequences. These elements were definitely present; the school's disciplinary practices were alive and well. Students were sometimes expelled from classrooms, suspended from school, sent to the dean's office to be written up for a variety of violations, and given punishments such as extra hours of study hall after school. Jason himself called the school a prison.

Though rules and prison-like surveillance were present, and often made life difficult for students, they were only the more obvious dimensions of student experience. Prisons, at least, are honest about their purpose, which is punishment. The bigger problem was that the school was not. It embodied a fundamental deception. The culture of contradiction told students they were being treated as adults, with free choice, freedom of speech, capacity to govern themselves, and capacity to engage in genuine learning. As a sign on the wall of one classroom read, "You live in the greatest country in the world because you get to express your freedom of choice." But this was a lie when it came to the reality of everyday practices. Jason saw this clearly: "They say they treat us like adults, but it's like a communistic country!"

The contradiction between expressed ideals and everyday practices was the greater problem, and it lay at the heart of the ordinary violence suffered by students and teachers alike. It operated most powerfully in the ways teachers taught, in the micro-interactions that constituted the events of learning each and every day. This was an education where procedures took the place of substance: where filling in the blanks, or putting numbers into boxes, or following a formula to write a paragraph or solve a physics problem, were confused with authentic teaching and learning. Without any opportunities for engaging in thinking at a deep level, students naturally disengaged. They "didn't get it" because there was, really, nothing to get.

Jason was, in his own words, "bored four or five hours a day." He put up with it all because he recognized the pull of life after school; he wanted to go to college. And school was the place where his friends were, where he could have a social life. As he said, "It's just survival. Just trying to get through the week. My philosophy is, you can win the battles, but you can't win the war."

With the impoverished intellectual opportunities offered to Jason and his peers, the end result was tension and a good deal of pain for everyone. Students used words like *painful* and *pure misery* to describe what school was like. Teachers struggled valiantly, but they were defeated by their own words and actions. They, too, needed to manage, to find ways to get through the stress of their days.

Rebel without a cause was an apt metaphor. Students were, in fact, rebels, acquiescent on one level with the daily routines, yet resisting in body and mind, often critical of the education they were receiving. But without a way to articulate the nature of that ordinary violence to which they were subject, they remained without a cause, and life went on as usual.

5

FROM QUIET RIOT TO REBEL WITHOUT A CAUSE

Continuity and Change in School

"You don't learn anything . . . "
"We don't learn nothing . . ."

Two students, twenty-six years apart. Two schools, three thousand miles apart.

And one critique.

What has changed in American schooling over the last thirty years? For sure, there *have* been many changes. Changing demographics in many parts of the country have completely transformed many previously all-white communities and schools into culturally diverse places. Bilingual and multicultural education, English-as-a-second-language education, special education, and gifted education, along with many other new developments and programs focused on raising student achievement have come to nearly every school in the country. State mandates for parental involvement, requirements for teacher certification and promotion, and new forms of accountability, including more standardized testing and state standards of learning, have dramatically transformed the school experience for many. Rising consciousness of crime and concerns for student safety, zero tolerance policies, and a host of other efforts to address school dropout problems have also greatly impacted schools.

With all these new developments in the educational policy, accountability, and organizational environments of schools, the question remains as to what impact, if any, they have had on the everyday, ordinary life of classrooms. Many scholars have argued that changing what teachers do is far more difficult. One reason is because practices surrounding teaching and learning are shaped by unexplored and unacknowledged aspects of culture—deeply held notions about what is normal, possible, and desirable that are highly resistant to change.

These notions constitute a script for teaching that governs the ways teachers ask questions, the things they do in the name of teaching, and their interpretations of and responses to student behavior. Structural changes may not only be irrelevant to daily life in classrooms, but they may in fact contribute to the ways classroom experiences for students *don't* change, in part because they focus attention on the superficial aspects of schooling and ignore the deep structures of talk and action that shape teaching.

Given the criticisms raised in earlier chapters of what was going on in Rick's and Jason's classrooms, it is very tempting to say quite simply that the teachers were incompetent, or even that the schools themselves were bad. Yet to do so would be to overlook a number of important truths: For one, both schools were highly regarded as "good schools" that sent large numbers of students on to college. Second, as far as teachers were concerned, it was clear that they were dedicated, sincere, and knowledgeable in their subject areas. Certainly they were individuals and brought their own personalities into their work. Some probably could have benefited from more professional development opportunities and more training. Yet none of them were considered "bad" teachers by their colleagues.

The more important point, however, was that their teaching was not purely idiosyncratic. It was a cultural activity, and thus in its basic form was shared by others and shaped by many unexplored assumptions, values, and patterns of behavior characteristic of the cultural system as a whole. The purpose of a cultural analysis is not to show how some teachers were bad, but to illustrate common themes and patterns. These do not reflect individual failings as such, but rather reflect the larger culture of teaching that shaped what all teachers did, more or less, in the classrooms Rick and Jason attended.

THE MORE THINGS CHANGE . . .

In 1983, Mr. B., Rick's biology teacher, said, "You'd better learn something so you can get a good job and get rich." As an average student, Rick did not have aspirations for college. Like most of his academically average peers, he just wanted to pass his courses so that he could be through with them, get out of school, and get on with his working life. His teachers reinforced this orientation toward the working world. There were constant accounting measures that emphasized getting the points and grades that would give the credentials you needed to get out of school and get a job.

In 2009, though, Jason, along with many of his other academically average peers, definitely did aspire to attend college. He was trying to get good enough grades and improve his standardized test scores so that he could get accepted. Among Rick and his peers, a clear shift toward the idea that college was for everyone channeled students away from vocational considerations toward the goal of higher education.

But Piedmont High was not preparing its average students such as Jason for college any better than Western was preparing its average students such as Rick. There have been numerous recent studies that have suggested that the "college for all" mentality has not delivered on its promise. Some have shown that while enrollment rates have increased, graduation rates in the United States have declined over time.[1]

Jason's motivation for college was financial: "Every hour I spend here is going to mean a thousand more dollars down the line." In that respect, he shared the school-equals-money equation that was prominent in Rick's classes, as well. The change was that high school was no longer enough in terms of its long-term financial reward. College was perceived as necessary for financial security. Though on the surface this was a change, at a deeper level the motivation and perceived value of education was similar: It was not about the development of the intellect, but about the return in cash.

STUDENT DISENGAGEMENT: GETTING BY AND GETTING THROUGH

The general terms of student disengagement, too, were remarkably similar over time: unopened books and notebooks (and, in 2009, backpacks) on desks, heads down on desks, tapping, drumming, doodling, note writing or other forms of non-classwork activity, talking, grooming, sleeping, and simply doing nothing. The one big change was that in 2009 there was more eating or snacking in class and more student and teacher circulation in and out of class. There also appeared to be more extraneous interruptions in classes in 2009, including (as noted in field journals) a variety of buzzers and bells, public announcements, and teacher phone calls.

What explains the increased circulation of student bodies in and out of classes? For one thing, the class periods in 2009 were roughly twice as long as those in 1983, due to the implementation of block scheduling. At the same time, teaching approaches had not changed all that much; what was boring in 1983 was still boring in 2009, it was just that there was more of it. Thus students needed ways to deal with the increased tension and frustration, and one of the only options was to get out of class in whatever way possible.

Another likely factor was the reduction in physical education class time. The amount of time Jason spent in his weight-lifting class was about one-third the amount of time that Rick had in his physical education classes. The denial of physical education likely had huge impacts on student well-being, leading to increased need to simply move to release mental, emotional, and physical tension. It was also possible that with increase in pull-out programs for special education, gifted education, or remedial instruction in 2009, students found themselves leaving class more often for other kinds of instructional activity, as well as visits to counselors or other school staff involved in managing student academic life.

Regardless of its cause, student circulation further contributed to the breakdown of an already fragile student learning experience. One might reasonably ask, how can classrooms and schools foster learning communities or support student focus and engagement with classroom activity when everybody, including teachers themselves, is constantly moving in and out? Interruptions in the form of announcements, bells, and phone calls also disrupted focus, making it harder for everyone to sustain interest and engagement over long periods of time.

INSTRUMENTAL AND PROCEDURAL TEACHING

Perhaps the most important continuity over time was in the ways teachers went about teaching. It goes without saying that teachers wanted students to be engaged with classroom learning and they worked hard to accomplish this. But one of the more prominent things they did, both in 1983 and 2009, was starting class by handing out worksheets or asking students to review quiz or worksheet questions, or copy a problem or exercise from the board.

In 2009, the problem seemed to have gone from bad to worse. One evolution of this was the "Do Now" exercise used in Jason's math and physics classes. These were apparently supposed to get students focused, thinking, and engaged with material, but in fact they accomplished the opposite of what they intended. They were signals to tune out, as was reflected quite eloquently one day when Jason stuffed his empty "Do Now" worksheet into his backpack.

Students carried around notebooks jammed with handouts (usually, in the case of males, in complete disarray). Unfortunately, the way in which worksheets and handouts mediated instruction in both schools virtually guaranteed that students would disengage, as paper-based activities, especially at the start of class, replaced face-to-face interaction between students and teachers.

Along with managing paper, in 1983 as in 2009, instruction was focused on rules or procedures for doing things. Both paper and procedures substituted for substantive engagement with content, meaning, or concepts. As I observed in Rick's English class, for example, though the class was reading a novel at the time, for two weeks there was a total of just fifteen minutes of discussion of the novel's themes. The rest of the class time was spent with the same list of twenty vocabulary words or in going over a mechanical model of what an essay should look like.

In another activity, students listened to a recording of a short story, but at the same time they were given an exercise sheet with specific questions to answer. They were told they would ". . . get all the answers right now" by listening to the recording. The story in itself was all but dismissed by converting it to a source of answers for an exercise. In Jason's English class there was marginally more time devoted to discussion of the novel's themes, and the teacher made valiant efforts to try to highlight important themes. Again, however, in both cases teachers ignored or dismissed important student ideas. In 1983 and 2009, the approach to teaching writing was similar, as well: In both cases students were presented with and expected to follow a formula for writing paragraphs.

In most classes the procedural nature of instruction made it seem like students were doing the same thing over and over again (and, in many cases, they were). Students clearly observed how repetitive the teaching was and considered that the education they were receiving was too slow and too simplistic, leading to comments such as, "We don't learn anything." The impoverished teaching itself demotivated students and had a profound effect on their engagement. A friend of Rick's said he was failing a math class he could readily pass just because of "the way the system is set up."

It is easy to see this as a defense mechanism on the part of an incapable student, but to do so would be to ignore what was really going on in classrooms, and the critiques that students themselves raised. Why should students be motivated to look for anything except a grade or points if they are not being offered anything of substance? At the same time, teachers thought that students couldn't handle the work, and so they systematically undermined their own efforts to engage them through a pedagogy based on deficit views of student capacities.

"YOU DON'T HAVE TO KNOW THIS": TEACHER SELF-DEFEAT

Telling students exactly what they needed to know for a test was a major way that teachers undermined their own efforts. The problem is that this approach, so eminently sensible on the one hand, also dismissed a good part of what they were doing in class as not necessary for students to know. The things that students found interesting and that could have been used to generate a deeper level of commitment and involvement in the subject as a whole were dismissed as unimportant and never included in the "real teaching," which was oriented toward the questions that would be on the test.

With the teachers' direct help, students learned early on to sort the stuff that mattered from the stuff that didn't. Mrs. S., Jason's physics teacher, repeatedly undermined herself by doing this; so did Mr. R., Mr. Stump, and Rick's teachers in 1983. Rick's Italian teacher, for example, after going through a number of drills that had effectively bored the entire class, told the class that only some of what he covered would be on the test, adding, "That's all I care about that you know. I don't care about the other [things]."

So why should students? Each time a teacher broached a topic of genuine interest to the class, they were told it would not be "on the test." The cumulative result was to stamp out any intrinsic enthusiasm for the subject(s). This was as true in 1983 (before the implementation of large-scale standardized testing) as it was in 2009. So it cannot be blamed on recent increases in standardized testing or teachers feeling they need to "teach to the test." They were doing this long before.

CONFUSING THE PROCEDURE WITH THE CONCEPT

An even greater difficulty was teachers' pervasive confusion of procedural-level teaching with higher-level concepts or ideas. Mr. Stump's factoring boxes, for example, were entirely procedural, yet he thought he was teaching "concepts." Mr. R.'s fill-in-the-blank teaching did little to advance student understanding of historical events. Mrs. S.'s endless repetition of step-by-step approaches to solving physics problems only served to perpetuate student confusion and did not advance students' conceptual understanding of the subject. In Rick's classes in 1983, too, drills, vocabulary lists, and the digestion of discrete facts were the heart of the curriculum

Why was this the case? Surely teachers realized that what they were actually doing was shooting themselves in the foot? In fact, though, they did not. More accurately, they *could* not, because the culture of teaching in which they were participants did not permit such awareness. It was built on a systemic contradiction between intents and practices that permeated everything from daily classroom behavior to the ways the institution itself characterized its mission (e.g., "Teachers are treating you like adults"). This contradiction resulted in an education that was largely a sham, since as long as the right intents and goals were present, there was no need to really look at whether practices were consistent with meeting them.

ORDINARY VIOLENCE: THEN AND NOW

A pedagogy of radical disconnect between the aims of education and the practices meant to achieve them lies at the heart of the ordinary violence of schooling as experienced by Rick and Jason. Though largely unacknowledged, it was keenly felt by students, who recognized the extent to which they were excluded from the teaching and learning that they were promised. Their disengagement was a completely rational and logical response. Students occasionally challenged this curriculum, but they did so through an underground and (from the schools' perspective) a largely invisible war: leaving comments on blackboards, muttering under their breath, engaging in small acts of defiance, or fighting battles with teachers over things such as water. Sometimes their discontent was manifest more dramatically in metaphors of pain and collapse.

Despite the overall similarities in classrooms over time, there was perhaps one major difference. In Rick's classes, student disengagement was a shared, almost collective act. There was a stronger sense of camaraderie among the students, more of a sense of solidarity, and more of a kind of "game playing" mentality that underlay their disengagement. One could see it readily in Rick's social studies class, his Italian class, and his biology class, as students joked among themselves and maintained strong connections with each other. The malaise students felt led them to want to get out of school, but it had not yet condensed into metaphors of pain and misery.

In Jason's classes, however, there was much less student solidarity. Though there were groups of friends in classes, there was less of a united front, as students disengaged individually, or waged private battles with teachers. The more individual nature of their suffering, perhaps, made it less bearable, and more painful. An increasingly individualistic ethos among students translated into more sharply defined individual experiences of suffering.

FROM THERE TO . . .

Rick and Jason were considered average students, and their experiences don't necessarily speak to the kind of instruction that one might find in honors-level classes or AP-level classes, or even other average-level classes in other schools. There were undoubtedly many unique features of school and classroom culture present in each setting. Eating in class may be tolerated in some schools; in others it may be forbidden. Rules and expectations will vary, and teachers themselves, being individuals, will also vary in important ways. School policies and climate will be different, and have differential impacts on student experiences.

At the same time, while unique in some respects, both schools and both experiences took place within a larger culture of schooling. Thus every classroom is in important ways like every other classroom, like some other classrooms, and like no other classroom.

The fact that students can sit through an entire class where instruction is simply a fill-in-the-blank exercise, or an endless repetition of fill in the boxes, means there is a need to look more closely at what schools are doing in the name of "education." Rick and Jason's classrooms are a mirror for an educational system that is not accomplishing what it sets out to do. They are not the whole story, but they can help us to see a very important part of the story.

6

ELEMENTARY MADNESS

"Hello, Mrs. Thomas, this is David's mom. Thanks for being my son's fourth-grade teacher. I saw on some information you sent home that you have placed my son in the Dolphins math group. I was just wondering what that means. How are the Dolphins different from the Sharks and the Otters? And I was also wondering how you decided to put him with the Dolphins? Thanks for any clarification you can provide."

"Dear Mrs. Hoffman, thanks for writing. We place all of our kids into different math groups so that we can best address their individual needs. We made these decisions based on their learning styles. The Dolphins are the kids who learn best from textbooks. Let me know if you have any further questions, and I look forward to working with you this year."

Hmmmm . . . Learning styles. Did they give the children a test to see what "learning style" they have? Are human beings, especially kids, locked in to learning in one particular way? A "textbook" learning style? Never heard of that. Maybe it means he can read. Or maybe it means he's not creative enough to "learn" through other methods. What about the Otters? Are they just going to get pictures to teach them math?

It is common for schools in the United States to test kids before they enter kindergarten with some kind of developmental screening test, supposedly to figure out which kids are coming into school already behind their peers and thus might be in need of additional remediation to catch up. What that also means is that even before setting foot in a school, a child is potentially already "at risk." Parents in some school districts cannot even enroll their children in school if they refuse to have them tested.

What about parents who aren't around to teach numbers and letters? Or whose kids don't visit libraries or have parents who tell them, "Use your words" when they get upset? Or who don't know enough to write the appropriate letters to the appropriate staff so that they can get the kind of class placements they want for their kids?

There is a grave social injustice buried deep in these practices, though it is hidden behind a powerful mythology of "individual needs." The discourse on individual needs in contemporary American schools reflects the unquestioned acceptance of individualized and psychological explanations for school failure and success. It constitutes the unwritten curriculum of schooling in America.

Parents believe that this is going to help their kids. Teachers, too, believe it; they are sincere in wanting to get kids the "help they need" to be successful. Producing "success for all" is a common goal of many schools in the country. But there cannot be "success for all" when the system is set up to produce success for some.

When schools place kids into academic levels or ability-tracked groups, they use nice words like "individualized education plans," "addressing individual needs," and "remediation." It's all about how kids themselves have deficiencies. Everybody is looking inside the heads of the kids to find the problems instead of into the practices of the classrooms and the school itself.

There are many educational researchers and teachers who firmly believe that if students fail to achieve in school, the problems lie in kids' families, their cultural differences, poverty, broken communities. Often, parents are blamed for their lack of involvement or support. A common refrain among teachers is, "We are doing the best job we can with the kids and parents we are getting." *Students* are penalized if *their parent* fails to sign a test.

In a society where families and their communities are already suffering from gross inequalities, how can anyone believe that tying kids' success to their parents' abilities and involvement will help to even things out? It's another way to avoid facing the truth about what is happening in schools themselves.

In fact, while every social and cultural system around the world is plagued with varying kinds of differences and social inequalities, some school systems are much better than others at compensating for these inequalities and producing higher levels of success for more students. Given equal levels of social problems or inequalities, the U.S. system as it is currently set up is one of the worst at leveling educational opportunities. In fact, the evidence shows that the U.S. system locks students into failure at higher rates than almost any system around.[1]

And yet the ideal of "success for all" is alive and well, and many educators and parents believe it. Survey after survey, parents say the schools their own children attend are doing a great job. (It's the *other* schools that aren't.)

It is ignorance about the everyday practices of schooling that permits these myths to survive in the face of massive evidence to the contrary. Until now this analysis has focused on high school classrooms. However, what happens at high school is not disconnected from what students experience during their earlier years of schooling. Indeed, what happens in high schools has its roots in the earliest grades. It is in these early grades that the educational trajectories of most everyone are set.

WOODLAND SCHOOL, FIRST GRADE, JANUARY 1998

It was 9 a.m., and the thirteen children in Mrs. John's first grade class were seated in a large circle on the floor. There were nine black children and four white children. The teacher was talking about how plants grow. As she did this, she confiscated a yo-yo toy from a black boy who was seated at the far side of the circle. Then she resumed a discussion of the calendar, weather, dates, seasons, and sunrise/sunset, returning to the plant theme at the end of her talk. Near the windows on one side of the classroom there were a few pots with bulbs sprouting.

After a few minutes' talk about the bulbs (importance of light, the growth cycle), the teacher transitioned to a reading activity called the "word wall," on which various words such as *people*, *because*, *did*, and *could* were written. During this activity, too, the teacher stopped to discipline another black boy, Brandon. "Is that what Mrs. Anna said not to bring to school?" Brandon showed the small toy he was holding. As the teacher left the classroom with him, he glanced back, looking sad.

While the teacher was absent with Brandon, the assistant teacher continued with the class. She asked students to read the words off the wall; then spell them; then put them in alphabetical order. The same two white girls answered nearly all of the questions, while the rest of the group sat fidgeting and looking around, paying little attention. The boys on the opposite side of the circle were completely disengaged from this activity.

After this, the TA instructed the kids to sit at their tables and put sets of word cards in alphabetical order. "I see some boys who might be losing a star," she warned. She handed the card sets to the white children in the class first.

The teacher returned to class with Brandon, and he went to sit at a small desk off to the side of the room, physically isolated from the rest of the class. Two other black boys also had separate desks. By now, all of the white kids and one black girl had their words organized, but the rest of the class had not even attempted the task. The TA was still in charge, as the teacher, after bringing Brandon back, left the room again.

The TA directed the kids to write their words in their composition books, under the first letter *W*, *P*, etc. As the noise level during this activity started to rise, the TA began saying repeatedly, "Shh . . . Shhhh . . ."

Interest in this activity soon waned, and many of the kids got up from their tables and went over to look at the potted bulbs again. The TA directed them to sit back down, but a black boy named Maurice got up again to spin the globe nearby. The TA said to him, "Excuse me? Are you finished?" The noise level rose as kids sat at the tables; few students had completed the activity.

As she collected the notebooks, the TA asked the kids again to quiet down . . . "Shhhh . . . Josh, please . . ." She began a countdown: "Five, four, three, two, one . . ." (a way, apparently, to get the kids to quiet down and transition to the next activity). She then started reading a story: *Animals in Wintertime*, a picture book about migration and hibernation. As kids moved from audible excitement at some points ("Wow!" when they learned a bird "flew all the way to Alabama") to boredom, noise and distraction levels rose again. The TA warned again, "Some people are just about ready to lose a star." (Each student's name was written on the board, with varying numbers of stars pasted underneath.)

While reading the story, she stopped again, a bit angry, to say, "I still see some people not paying attention! Sit up, Josh!" Maurice was still at the globe, spinning it slowly. Maurice, along with three other black boys, Jamal, Nicholas, and Brandon, all had separate desks in the "satellite" area.

After the story was done, the TA announced, "I'm gonna give you a paper, and your job is just to put your name on it. . . . Brandon, take the paper. Sit down—that's not a big job to do. Just put your name on the paper where it says, 'Name.'" Maurice spelled out Joshua's name.

Some students started cutting the paper, but then she said, "I have not asked you to cut anything at all! I'm gonna give you glue and then I'm gonna let you cut." She stood at the board. "I don't see everybody's eyes. . . . Okay, let's read the instructions together. . . . 'Cut out . . .'" But many of the kids had already begun cutting. The task was to cut out pictures and glue them into place on the worksheet. As the students did this, she went over to Brandon and glued his for him. "Somebody's making noise!" she said. Nicholas was playing with the glue.

As this activity began to wind up, she tried to engage the students in a discussion. "Raise your hand if you can tell me what a squirrel does to get ready for winter?" She simultaneously disciplined misbehaving students, telling them, "Pencils down—put your hands in your lap." Nicholas was still cutting and gluing. She offered a story about hitting a deer at night, and Brandon was immediately attentive, raising his hand to ask permission to talk. He could hardly wait to be called on, though, and he started talking about a rabbit, at which point the TA reprimanded him, telling him to put his hand down. He kept it up, however, and continued talking: "I wanted to tell a story. . . . My uncle shot a deer . . . ," but the TA just ignored him. This discussion was cut short as the TA finally said, "Now we're gonna have snack time."

The satellite kids' chairs have squares marked in masking tape around them. During snack time, a number of kids (including Brandon) got up and went over to the potted bulbs again, as Beethoven's "Moonlight Sonata" played from a cassette recorder. The TA told Brandon to get away from the bulbs. Maurice was standing in front of a poster counting loudly from one to twenty, and Brandon asked, "When are we going to PE?"

She replied, "Five more minutes. . . ." And then she handed out another worksheet. Nicholas said, "I'm not doing nothin'." The TA then said, "I can't hear the music very well," in reference to the growing noise level. Maurice and Brandon were at the bulbs again.

Noticing this, she said, "If you're over at the plants, you need to come and sit down. . . . I'm gonna check if you have your name on your paper." She then saw that Nicholas was still cutting something out. "What is it you are cutting?" She also asked Kristen, "Why is this paper like this?" as she saw that Kristen had cut out some small shapes on the edge of the worksheet.

It was now time to line up to go to PE. "If you're in line and you're talking, you sit down."

In some respects, this first grade classroom was quite ordinary. Both kids and teachers were engaged in activities one might find in any first grade classroom in the United States: children sitting in a circle on the floor, story time, word exercises, an art project. Teachers exerted efforts to keep the kids quiet and focused, and enforced rules regarding prohibited items. A behavioral reward system (stars) was also in place. None of these things stands out as particularly unique.

Yet if one explores this classroom through a cultural lens, a number of interesting themes emerge. Kids were being taught many unintended lessons about who succeeds and who doesn't, about the contradictions embedded in education, about disengagement, and about the ways in which the classroom itself sets kids up for failure, despite the teachers' best intentions.

One of the more powerful contradictions embedded in this classroom concerned student engagement. While many of the students were already disengaged for much of the time, they were still part of the group and were able to function as such. However, the black boys experienced much stronger ostracization—they each had individual desks in the outer periphery of the room, well apart from the tables where most students sat. On the floor around each desk was a square drawn in masking tape, further marking off these students as somehow different.

The great irony, of course, was that these boys, who were being ostracized, were the ones with the most enthusiasm. They were completely engaged—but with the one thing that the teacher would not let them engage with—the bulbs! The battle of the bulbs reflected the paradox of a pedagogy that values student engagement but that systematically defeats it in practice. Both teachers and students were bound up in this paradox: that the one thing that really grabbed kids' attention—the one genuine source of life in the classroom—was off-limits. The deeper lesson for the boys was a lesson in contradiction: Things are not what they seem to be. People tell you to be involved, they seem to value your participation, then they systematically prevent you from pursuing it. It was something of a catch-22: damned if you do, damned if you don't.

The long-term result can be seen in the high school classrooms, where black students experienced very high levels of alienation, even more so than white students. In Jason's classes, teachers didn't even bother to wake the black students when they were sleeping. It was a long process of extinction, undoubtedly repeated time and again: Don't bother engaging, because your enthusiasm won't be tolerated or respected no matter what you do.

This contradiction had another unfortunate consequence. Brandon, Nicholas, Josh, and Maurice's identities were already being cemented as "at risk." Their physical separation from the other students was one all-too-obvious clue. All of their activities were highlighted, almost as if everything they did was under a spotlight. They were inordinately targeted by the teacher for comments about noise levels and for "engaging" in activities that were peripheral to the main activity of the classroom (looking at the bulbs, spinning the globe, cutting/gluing paper). They had lots of enthusiasm, but it was recast as a disciplinary problem.

The activities that the children were asked to engage in, too, contributed to student disengagement. For one thing, there was no coherence among the many different activities the children were exposed to. Talking about the bulbs was followed up with a word wall activity that asked kids to read random words and then spell them. Then kids were instructed to do an alphabetizing/sorting activity with cards, followed by writing the same words in their composition books. This was followed by a story about animals in winter, then a worksheet collage. There was no apparent connection between the bulbs, the word activities, the story about animals, and the worksheet. This piecemeal approach itself prevents students from developing sustained interest or finding their enthusiasm connected to deeper and broader meanings of a subject.

Further, throughout this period, even these activities themselves were punctuated by negative disciplinary interruptions: the confiscated yo-yo during the bulbs discussion, Brandon with his "toy" during the word wall, the constant "Shhhh" reminders during the word sort and story reading, the constant requests for kids to stop looking at the bulbs, the warnings about "some kids losing a star," the requests to sit down, sit up, stop the globe spinning, the paper cutting, the gluing. And even the efforts of kids to contribute to the discussion were cause for disciplinary action, as Brandon tried to share his story and was ignored. The constant negative discipline further undermined any positive emotional connection students might have had to the content or to the class as a community.

Another powerful form of interruption consisted of movement in and out of classrooms. Kids were taken out of class, as was Brandon, whose toy became a cause for disciplinary removal. The teacher circulated, too; after disciplining Brandon, and then returning with him to class, Mrs. John left the classroom again for almost the entire period. Whether it was teachers who moved, or kids, for whatever reasons—the end result was the same: a loss of connection, both to the group as a community and to the substantive activity of the class. Remarkably, the same pattern of circulation was present in high schools, to an even greater degree.

The ultimate irony, however, was that even when kids did things "right," they ended up doing them "wrong." During the worksheet/cutting exercise, kids knew what they had to do—cut out the pictures—and they plunged right in. But this ended up being the wrong thing to do, as the teacher said, "I have not asked you to cut anything at all. . . ." On the surface, the whole activity appeared to be about student creativity through cutting and gluing, but the real, unspoken lesson was rule-following and compliance with teacher directives.

What was supposed to be fun became an occasion for reprimand. Once again, kids were punished for their enthusiasm, instead of being rewarded for it. No wonder children felt frustrated. They were supposed to be involved, active learners, and they had both the energy and the will to be, but at every moment their enthusiasm and involvement was recast as "disruptive." This was a form of deception, albeit one that was completely invisible to the teacher.

This process was particularly evident for the black boys, whose actions constantly drew reprimand and sanction. By contrast, the kids who managed most successfully to stay under the radar were the girls, both white and black, but especially the white girls. They were the ones who answered all the teachers' questions in the right way at the right time; they were the ones who got the word cards first. So even here in the first grade one can see the roots of the later disparities that will afflict school performance across gender and racial divides.

But some kids were also already learning to express their discontent with the status quo. The kids' constant attraction to the potted bulbs, despite teacher warnings that they stay away, could be read that way. Maurice, too, as he stood spinning the globe (another cause for disciplinary attention), beginning a countdown till the end of class, gave a clear message that he wanted out. Brandon actually spoke up, asking, "When are we going to PE?" And Nicholas, seeing that the teacher was handing out another worksheet just as class was ending, voiced his (very reasonable) refusal, saying, "I'm not doing nothin'."

While it is important to recognize that school is a place where kids need to learn to adapt to the demands of a classroom, sometimes those demands create more problems than they need to. When they deceive children as to the true nature of the activities they are engaged in, and when they fail to harness children's own enthusiasm and desire to learn, they work against kids rather than for them. When they end up ostracizing and marginalizing some kids and not others, they also work against all children's best interests.

Couldn't the class activity be organized differently to build on children's enthusiasm and interest, instead of converting it into an occasion for disciplinary action? Of course it could. The teacher in this classroom, for example, could have structured an entire class around the potted bulbs, engaging students in a genuine fashion and harnessing their clear excitement, and in the same time create a deeper, more internally coherent curriculum. Couldn't teachers find ways to create a classroom community without ostracizing kids? Of course they could; the black boys in this class did not have to sit at satellite desks with masking tape squares drawn around them to further symbolize their non-belonging. Couldn't activities be delivered without hijacking their intended purpose? Of course; there's no reason to convert an intrinsically interesting art activity into a lesson in impulse control. But that would demand a critical inquiry into the classroom experiences of children and a willingness to confront the ways that current practices do not serve children or teachers well.

In this first grade classroom, we can already see the seeds of disengagement, risk, frustration, and poor pedagogy being sown. Though educators talk endlessly about addressing individual needs, in fact the individual needs of kids like Brandon and Maurice are not being addressed. For what kids such as Brandon "need"—and they are not alone—are the very things they are being excluded from: positive recognition and connection with the life of the classroom. In this respect, the discourse and practice of an education built on individual needs is thus another form of inauthentic education, because the true nature of those needs is never understood. Brandon and Maurice were not disengaged non-learners. But they were learning to be such, because the institution itself was constructing them along those lines.

Because it cannot align its goals with its practices, the classroom, through its pedagogy, ends up defeating its own purposes. Both teachers and children are trapped in this contradiction: Teachers, because they are by definition delegates of the institution, are tasked with enforcing its demands and following its scripts, all the while perhaps feeling frustrated with the firsthand experiences that belie the goodness and effectiveness of those scripts. Children are trapped because no matter how hard they try, the messages they get are contradictory: what is good is also what is bad, and the things one is asked to do are not what they seem. Who would not be frustrated?

Is change possible? Of course it is. But unless we recognize the internal paradoxes that afflict the ways we construct classrooms, we can't begin to address the ways in which we could transform them into places that truly do the things we say we want them to do.

7

TOWARD AUTHENTIC SCHOOLING

Letter Home to the Parents of Fourth Graders:

". . . Through a fairly structured regimen in both science and social studies, your child will produce several major research papers. . . ."

What happens when individuals in an organization such as a school, despite their best efforts, act in ways that belie their intentions? On the one hand, it is easy to offer an individualistic explanation that blames teachers for not being better at their jobs. It's also common to look for explanations in the forces outside of school—poverty or family dysfunction, for example—that impinge on schools and affect students in negative ways.

What we lack is a perspective that focuses on the daily interactional contexts that make up the school and the classroom. It is in these contexts that meanings are made and where patterns of behavior take on life and significance. Certainly individuals are imperfect, and there is never any seamless match between what people understand about themselves and claim as their goals and desires and what they do in real time. Yet what happens when this pattern becomes intrinsic to the culture of a school?

More news from the fourth grade:

Dear Parents,

This week the students have been much more focused and settled as a whole. However, there are still several problem areas, one of which is homework. . . . In your child's assignment book, you will find a note from Mr. Farmer and me. It tells you whether your child came prepared and ready to learn each day. . . . If the homework is reading a selection in the Social Studies or Science book, please help your child by listening to him or her read. Those textbooks are extremely difficult for most of the children, and they could use your support to be successful. . . .

This week, we have reread the first section in the Science book on electricity and held several conversations about it. One day I went home bragging just how much these kids knew about that section, because they had literally had it as homework, reread it silently in class, reread it aloud as a class, and we had gone over the material in another class discussion. I thought they had it down pat. They could answer any question I asked, they could define the words in that section, and they could talk intelligently about the facts and concepts they had learned.

However, and this is one of the prime examples of students' learning needs, we had an exploratory science lesson yesterday with bulbs, batteries, and wires, and they were asked to first predict some ways to connect the thee objects to light the bulb. (They had seen pictures in the book, remember, and they could also define circuit.) Not one bulb got lit. So we went over the factual info they had studied previously. . . . And we tried again, but not one bulb got lit. . . .

Our time was over, so we collected our materials. Today's lesson is NOT going to be exploratory, but instead, directed. They obviously did not make the connection between what they knew intellectually and the materials they had to use. . . . But when they are not successful, they need to have the support [from home] to be successful. . . . Your help from home, in making sure your child is prepared and ready to learn when they arrive at school, is CRUCIAL for success. . . . I know YOU want the best for your child. We, too, want the best learning situation possible for your child, so consider volunteering in our room, and if you can't do that, please check your child's work nightly.

Probably many parents and teachers would find such a letter unremarkable. How often have we heard that parent involvement is essential for a student's educational success, or that parents need to be partners with their children's teachers in supporting student achievement? Parents who are not checking their child's homework and who are not reading with their kids are not doing enough to make sure their kids come to school "ready to learn." In this classroom it was the parents who were failing, and this led to the kids' lack of success.

However, when we consider what the teacher had to say about her own approach to teaching, it was possible that parents (or "unready" kids, for that matter) had little to do with the kids' evident lack of success. It was the teacher's failure to teach effectively. In fact, she went about teaching this unit in exactly the *wrong* way. Instead of starting with hands-on activity and then moving to a conceptual explanation, she started with the concepts and then tried to get students to apply them in a hands-on activity. This was a teacher with twenty-six years of experience who had actually won an award for being among the best science teachers in the state.

This is the way many teachers in the United States still go about teaching, by first presenting "the concepts" (if they are even that), and then having students try to apply them to real problems. More effective teaching reverses this order. Comparative studies of science teaching in Taiwan and Japan, for example, reveal that teachers tend to present students with a real-life problem first, and have students generate their own solutions. In this way, their conceptual understanding emerges from authentic engagement with a problem-solving process.[1]

A further difficulty was that this teacher apparently thought that reading about electric circuits, and being able to define words and answer questions and talk about circuits, was the same thing as having a real conceptual understanding of electric circuits. Conceptual-level engagement was confused with textual, verbal, and procedural forms of engagement. This is another version of the same problem seen in Jason and Rick's high school classes, where lower-order mechanical or procedural tasks replaced conceptual engagement with subject matter.

The final irony was that the teacher cast the whole event as a "prime example of students' learning needs," falling back on the cultural discourse of individual deficit. This discourse, so powerful and popular among educators in the United States, allows educators to avoid really looking at classroom teaching in any depth, since it already assigns problems elsewhere—especially to individual lacks or deficits.

A closer consideration of classroom pedagogy (here revealed only in the letter home, unfortunately, not in firsthand observation) suggests that kids' failure to achieve was probably not their parents' fault, or the fault of the kids themselves for "not being ready." It was the result of poor teaching. One might also consider this as a case of *inauthentic* teaching. Inauthentic teaching occurs whenever there is a split between the goals of learning and the activities or practices of teaching.

The idea that student difficulties are *individual*, due to "needs" or some other deficiency in the person, is the dominant lens shared by many parents and teachers. It is one support for inauthentic teaching, since it directs attention away from examination of the teaching process toward other extraneous factors.

A simple case of this is the textbooks, which the teacher claimed were "far too difficult" for students to read on their own. If it was inappropriate textbooks that created needy students, why not get better textbooks? Why translate the whole situation into a discourse about students needing parental support? This is an example of an institutional-level problem that gets redefined in terms of individual needs.

The cumulative result of the cultural habit of locating problems in individual students ("needs") or in their parents' lack of involvement ("failure to support") is that classroom practices escape critical inquiry. Certainly the teacher was sincere; she was simply using the dominant frame for explanation of educational problems shared by many educators and parents in the United States. This framework strongly privileges individual needs and parent involvement as the right ways to look at education.

Arguing against an overly individualized lens or an overly structural lens on student achievement does not dismiss the effects of cultural and socioeconomic influences outside the school on what happens to students inside the school. Much research reminds us that schooling always exists in a particular social context, and that this context has a powerful effect on individual student outcomes.

It is precisely because of this context that requirements for parent involvement are problematic. There are already vast inequalities in the kinds of resources and other forms of social and economic support that are available to parents. For families with two working parents, single parent households, less economically advantaged households, and cultural and racial minority households, making student success so dependent on parent involvement is bound to disadvantage those students whose parents can't be "involved" in the right ways. Rather than leveling the playing field as much as possible, making parent involvement necessary to student success exacerbates the social inequalities that already exist, as parents with more social and cultural capital have distinct advantages in supporting their children's school success.[2]

Looking at the situation from an even wider lens, there is evidence that shows that schools in the United States, compared to those of other nations, do a far worse job of compensating for relative social disadvantage. That is to say, students from disadvantaged backgrounds in the United States are more likely to experience school failure than similarly disadvantaged students in other nations.[3]

There are many factors that go into this (notably the persistence of early academic-level tracking in U.S. schools), but increasing the role that families play in education, within a system that already magnifies the impact of socioeconomic inequalities, is surely one route to exacerbating inequitable outcomes rather than alleviating them.

Ironically, there is not a school in the country that does not aspire to "Success for All," the motto of the school district where Jason went to school. And yet, as the experiences of Brandon and his friends show, even in the best of schools, from the earliest grades classrooms are sites where some students are already being selected for failure. This happens not through conscious intent, but through instructional and regulatory practices that are internally contradictory, and whose effects are magnified for those students already marked by differences of race and social class.

AN AUTHENTIC EDUCATION?

In recent years, there has been a push for what some have called authentic education. In the usual sense of the term, *authentic education* connects what students are learning in school to the real world outside the school. It means giving students what have been called real-world problem-solving skills, or, alternately, to foster student learning by doing. Often it is about making classroom learning relevant to the twenty-first century. It may also include assessments that supposedly give a more complex and holistic picture of students' abilities and knowledge than multiple choice or paper and pencil tests.

As it is used here, the term *authentic education* means something different. It is not so much about the match between what goes on inside the classroom and the supposed "real world" outside (after all, the classroom is just as "real"), but about fidelity between the intent or goals of an educational endeavor and the practices meant to achieve them. Even a supposed "real world" problem-solving exercise can be inauthentic if in the process of adaptation to the classroom, it is translated into superficial procedural or organizational kinds of activities. Authenticity in the sense used here is thus more importantly about fidelity to purpose than about specific questions of content or relevance.

Obviously, this interpretation does not negate the desirability of relevance and "real world" applications and connections. Nor does it guarantee that the goals or intents are well thought out or appropriate. Those remain important dimensions of a good education. But for goals to be reached in the first place, they must be authentically present or accessible via the activities and practices meant to embody them.

Seen through this lens, the kind of schooling provided to students such as Rick, Jason, and Brandon was inauthentic. Teachers misrecognized their own activities, and the school itself contributed to an environment of misrecognition by failing to practice what it preached (e.g., "We are treating you like adults . . ."). Inauthentic education can happen many ways—by substituting procedural activity for conceptual engagement, by promoting inflated representations of student and teacher activity ("major research papers"), by undermining students' connections with subject matter, or by simultaneously advocating one goal but defeating it in practice with another. The result is an impoverished and superficial pedagogy.

An authentic education, on the other hand, engages both students and teachers in the heart of the subject matter at hand. In authentic instruction, there are no students who are not "ready to learn." Instead of seeing individuals as deficient, or blaming difficulties on forces outside the classroom, it places the spotlight on the classroom itself, and especially on how instructional practices enable or impede student connections to subject matter.

As a construct to explore classroom teaching and learning, authentic education does not blame teachers as individuals, for it recognizes that their difficulties go beyond any one individual. Teachers are participants in a larger culture that makes available to them ideas such as individual needs and deficiencies. This larger culture also shapes the ways goals are translated or mistranslated into curricular practices. If teachers consistently misrecognize themselves and their activities, it is not because they are bad people or incompetent teachers, but because the culture itself fosters contradictions between what it says and what it does.

CONNECTING INAUTHENTIC EDUCATION AND [ORDINARY] VIOLENCE

School violence has been the subject of intense research and prevention efforts in the United States. Most of the time, the causes of violence, like those of underachievement, are seen to lie in students themselves or in their families or communities, or in policies that make weapons readily available, for example. Mental and emotional illness, drug use, dysfunctional families, poverty, availability of weapons, community breakdown—all have been identified as proximate causes of school violence.

Yet, contrary to this view, international studies have shown that patterns of violence in schools are not predicted by levels of individual mental health or what is going on outside of the schools. That is to say, individual, societal, family, or community factors are insufficient to predict and understand school violence. Rather, as the work of David Baker and Gerald LeTendre has shown, violence is strongly connected to conditions *within* schools themselves, and in particular to the *quality of education* students receive.[4]

U.S. debates on school violence have overlooked the importance of ordinary instructional experiences of students and the cumulative effect of these on educational quality. While the schools described in this book were not violent places in the usual sense of the term, they were sites of ordinary violence in which profound disconnection, disengagement, and frustration characterized student experiences. Disengagement was not a simple "choice" that an individual student made. It was powerfully normalized in ordinary classroom interactions and practices that systematically removed opportunities for intellectual engagement with subject matter.

Students realized that they were being lied to: They were not getting the education that the school told them they were getting, or that was held up in the superficial discourses of teaching/learning that infused their days at school. Read in this way, the school's deception was a form of institutionalized ordinary violence. Expressions of pain and suffering among students spoke to the larger and deeper disruption that underlay the very promises of the institution itself. Student disengagement was thus a logical expression of frustration and even anger that students felt at being deceived. It was not an act of uncaring; in fact, it was the opposite.

Does this ordinary violence, embedded in the practices and discourses of the school, connect in some way with "real" violence? There is as yet little research on ordinary violence in schools, and thus no evidence to support a direct, causal link between ordinary violence and beatings, shootings, bullying, or other forms of physical violence. Yet if we consider how international evidence illustrates a link between violence and the quality of education students receive, we can then begin to consider how the ordinary practices of school can create an environment conducive to more egregious forms of overt violence.

RETHINKING AUTHENTIC EDUCATION AND PERSONHOOD IN CONTEXTS OF ORDINARY VIOLENCE

Saying that fourth graders might be "producing several major research papers" may appeal to some parents, as it represents fourth graders and their teacher as being serious and competent. Yet at a time when even college students have trouble with writing even one research paper, it seems a bit inflated to say that fourth graders will be producing four major ones. Inflated discourses about teaching and learning make teachers and parents feel good, but the end result is that everyone needs to jump on the bandwagon of self-promotion, otherwise one risks simply becoming invisible. Ordinariness is now a form of deficiency.

But when the demands for self-inflation become systemic, constant, and integrated into the core of educational processes, the consequences are different. This is because selves and identities lie at the core of an educational experience. There is no learning in the absence of a concomitant shaping of an identity. When those identities are educated in the context of inflated or inauthentic representations of their own activity, they themselves develop in inauthentic ways.

Aside from its consequences in ethical and moral domains, this is a form of violence against persons. If people are pressured to represent themselves in distorted, inflated, or self-important terms, they cannot develop the capacity to see themselves or others for who or what they are. A pervasive climate of obfuscation and misrepresentation develops, which is the very antithesis to the goals and ideals of a moral, democratic, and socially just education.

The institution was not honest about its purposes, either. It promised an "education for all," but it was most certainly not available to all. It might have been available to honors students, and maybe even to special education students, but not to students such as Rick and Jason. Their identities as "average" students were invisible. The only time they became visible was when surveillance detected that they had violated rules. This, too, was a form of ordinary violence, directed against the persons of students, that denied their identities as learners.

CHANGING THE CULTURE OF SCHOOLING

The fact that there was such continuity over time in the classrooms experienced by Rick and Jason illustrates the robust nature of school culture in the face of many outside pressures for change. Schools haven't changed in fundamental ways because change efforts have not focused on the ways of thinking and behaving that constitute the deep cultural practices of school. Instead, ever more emphasis is being placed on the procedural, managerial, and programmatic aspects of schooling. These make it even harder to focus on the things that really matter: the realities of classroom life.

So how might we go about producing the kinds of changes that would enable students such as Rick, Jason, and Brandon to experience an education that is intellectually engaging and authentic in the deepest sense of that term?

It is easier to say what will not work: more emphasis on testing, more accountability, more remedial classes, more workshops, more time on task, smaller classes, longer school years, more social-emotional curricula, more citizenship lessons, etc. All of these efforts, while undoubtedly able to produce *some* successes in *some* cases, do not radically reinvent the culture of schooling.

However, it is also true that cultures do change, and sometimes they can be changed in intentional ways. The entire history of education is a story of cultural change, of the flow of ideas and practices across boundaries of time and space. Sometimes changing behavior and action is key to changing meaning, values, and attitudes; sometimes the latter change first and practices follow.

The following ideas are ways to think about generating deeper and more impactful transformation in the culture of schools and classrooms.

1. *Educate teachers to really see their own practices*. This should be done in programs for pre-service teacher education, of course, but it can also be done in schools themselves. Most teacher education programs already incorporate mentoring and peer evaluation, including classroom observations and evaluations. Anyone who is a teacher or who has been through a teacher education program is quite familiar with this process.

   But as it is usually done in U.S. schools of education, these approaches do not radically transform the ways teachers *see* themselves and their practices. Observations are typically done using a checklist; or, if not, observations are coded using predetermined terms or categories. The terms of analysis are already familiar and accepted within the culture of teaching. This does not allow new ideas or new perceptions to emerge, nor does it really allow us to discover the important patterns of interaction and meaning that exist beneath the superficial tasks and activities of classroom life.

   Instead, educators need to learn to see classrooms the way anthropologists see them, as cultural environments with patterns of behavior and interaction that require *discovery*. Every setting has an inner cultural logic—a set of deeply held values and meanings that govern what people say and do in a given place and time. This logic is manifest in the interactions as well as in the physical environment; they are interconnected.

However, this cultural logic functions largely implicitly; people use it but are not necessarily aware of it. If teachers and other educators had the skills to really see classrooms as places where such logic has a powerful effect on what they can accomplish, they could begin to see their practice with new eyes and generate new approaches to change.

This could be done by making apprenticeships in ethnographic observation a requirement in all teacher education programs and by creating grass-roots movements among teachers for developing their own in-service teaching observation and analysis groups (see #6 below). Models for this exist already; one such effort involves adapting Japanese educators' cultural practices surrounding "Lesson Study" in U.S. schools. This is also an approach that is highly compatible with online technologies.[5]

2. *Internationalize teacher education at a fundamental level by incorporating evidence on teaching and schooling from around the world.* One of the best ways to get people to see themselves more accurately is to confront them with differences. This needs to be done in a way that is more than just an "exposure" to different approaches to teaching, but a deep encounter that requires them to understand the larger conceptual and cultural logics that inform teaching and learning. The work of Joseph Tobin and colleagues, for example, is based on videos of classrooms in Japan, China, and the United States; by showing videos of classrooms in each country to teachers, parents, and students in the other countries, they were able to generate critical discourses on deep levels of teaching as a cultural activity.[6] While their work was focused on research, a similar approach could be used in teacher education programs. Video archives on classrooms and teaching from around the world should be shared and used to generate new discourses and debates on what is done in teaching.

3. *Create an alternative discourse on reform by engaging students more visibly and actively in educational research and reform initiatives.* Putting students' views and perspectives at the center of reform is essential if we are to generate genuine change in

education. Too much discussion about education occurs in the absence of genuine student input. Even young children should be given more visibility and presence in research, most powerfully through child-centered ethnographic work that treats children as participating subjects, not simply as "objects" of research. This perspective aligns with recent movements in childhood studies that privilege children's agency and voice.

Of course, this is not easy, given the way research is currently conducted in and on education and the lack of a powerful voice and presence for students and youth. There are also some serious difficulties involved in work that intends to privilege voice and agency of children and youth but co-opts this into adult-centric ideological agendas. But there are promising practices, including ethnographic and participant action research, that have been used with youth and could be incorporated into the training that educators receive.

4. *Disengage from polarizing discourses on schooling, society, and education, and put the focus back on the classroom.* Values, ethics, and politics are important, but not if they are disembodied from real practices in classrooms and schools. In fact, one of the best ways to approach debates on these topics is through the lens of everyday classroom practices. We face a pervasive climate of blame in discussions of education that usually targets different groups of actors (teachers, parents, political actors and organizations, or students themselves) or, alternatively, problems of society at large (such as poverty, racial discrimination). This polarization does little to address the realities of everyday practices in schools and classrooms, the real contexts that shape immediate experiences of teaching and learning. It is in these contexts that people are far more capable of appreciating the need for change and the possibility of change.

5. *Make concrete administrative and organizational changes in ways that can have substantive impact on classroom experiences.* Every teacher or administrator should spend a few days going through the school day in order to appreciate what it is like from the student's perspective. This is because what is important to change can't be decided in advance without real firsthand knowledge of

everyday experiences of students. Things that could be changed include block scheduling, timing of breaks and lunch periods, constant bells and other interruptions, practices surrounding pulling students out of class, disciplinary practices (e.g., zero tolerance policies, suspensions, overly restrictive rules, etc.), useless "study halls," and other practices that affect student and teacher movement into and out of classes. Of course, given the nature of large public schools and policies decided on district and state levels, some of these changes need to be made at a systemic level. But a dialogue about the need for change is a first step, and it has to be generated from the ground up in ways that speak to the authentic experiences of students.

6. *Make participation in teacher and administrator self-inquiry and research groups an integral part of what it means to be an educator.* This would go a long way toward generating a climate of openness to change. Teacher research groups are autonomous groups of educators who decide on a problem or focus that is significant in their own situation. In a sense, what this means is that teachers develop inquiry into their own practice and generate understandings, ideas, and solutions for problems that are immediately and powerfully linked to their own contexts. In fact, some studies of teacher-researcher groups have shown that these groups can have a powerful effect on teaching and learning, most importantly by addressing the gap that exists between goals and real practices—a central problem identified in the previous chapters. According to Kenneth Zeichner at the University of Wisconsin, Madison, who conducted an analysis of teacher research groups, teachers report that they become more learner-centered in their practice, and their assumptions about themselves and their practices become more open to change, with positive effects on school culture.[7]

7. *Change the discourse and practices surrounding discipline and violence in schools.* Violence exists whenever cultural or social processes systematically deny the humanity and capability of those they are supposed to serve. It is not a problem that can be controlled through more physical restraints and surveillance, more disciplinary sanctions, more add-on programs. All of these measures address the performances of violence without addressing its

roots, which lie rather in the ordinary practices of doing school and in the quality of the teaching and learning process.

We can make classrooms and schools into places that honor the powerful urge to engage with the world around us by more attention to the ways in which those connections are supported or undermined in everyday activities. Students and teachers are frustrated by failures to connect; they search for causes in students themselves or in their families or society. Certainly problems exist in all of those domains, but it is in the ordinary practices of classroom interactions and instruction that we can find opportunities for reconnection.

If the roots of violence are reframed as a problem of connection, not of more control over student bodies that are in a deep sense already overcontrolled, we may have a basis for changing schools in a direction that supports more humanity for everyone.

8. *Listen to the "others."* The "others" are all those who are marginal and/or marginalized—students, many from different racial and ethnic groups, who are present in schools but never really given much attention (except when they become academic or behavioral "problems"); cafeteria workers, janitors, part-time volunteers. These persons, whose presence is so integral to the functioning of a school, are more often than not ignored. Others can also include white students who are "at risk" or otherwise considered in need—to use that felicitous phrase heard at Jason's school—of a "jump start."

As my research on Iranian students in a Los Angeles High School in the early 1980s suggested, outsiders to the system have extremely valuable critical perspectives to share on what goes on in schools. Long before "caring" became a prominent theme in educational research and thinking about teaching, for example, Iranian students were voicing their pointed critiques about what they perceived as their U.S. teachers' failure to care. They experienced the gaps firsthand between what teachers claimed they were doing in classrooms and what they were really practicing.

Yet talk about reform rarely prioritizes or even incorporates the perspectives of the marginalized. When the latter do attempt to become active agents in educational critique and change, they face enormous obstacles to having their views recognized and treated as legitimate.[8]

Instead of dismissing minority voices, we should be listening to them and taking their views seriously, because their very marginality is a rich resource. As anthropologists know well, being on the periphery enables one to see more, since one is not already caught up in taken-for-granted meanings and assumptions that dominate the mainstream.

ENVISIONING THE FUTURE

The institutions that shape our understanding of what it means to educate—namely, universities and institutions of higher education—have a responsibility to generate new ways of thinking and talking about education. It is in these spaces that teachers are prepared and where a new generation of teachers and learners can emerge. It is vitally important that a new discourse about learning and teaching evolve that avoids the tired pitfalls of polarizing individual versus societal explanations for "failure."

We need the skills and the will to look at the situations we create on a daily basis in order to address the reality of what school means to the people involved in it. It is here where we can begin to connect our visions of and for education with the practices that we engage in.

Far into the future, perhaps, classrooms and schools as we know them will be obsolete. We will wonder why we agonized over the small things, when the very institution of school is destined for radical reformulation. But for now, it is the small things, the daily stuff of classrooms, that offer the best and boldest windows on possibilities for change.

NOTES

INTRODUCTION

1. See Gerry Rosenfeld (1971), *"Shut Those Thick Lips!": A Study of Slum School Failure* (New York: Holt, Rinehart, and Winston).

2. Basing his ideas on the philosophy of John Dewey, Elliot Eisner developed the notion of "educational connoisseurhsip" to encourage deeper inquiry into the practices of schooling, trusting individuals with the capacity to develop new eyes to see and critique education.

3. See David Tyack, a well-known historian of education, who discusses the question in his 1997 book, *Tinkering Toward Utopia* (Cambridge, Harvard University).

4. This is known in philosophy as the hermeneutic circle. Interpretations always move from part to whole and back; the parts reflect on the whole and the whole depends on the parts.

5. See Clifford Geertz, 1985.

6. This is also true for the "hard" sciences, such as physics, for example.

7. For example, see LeVine and Norman (2001), who have studied attachment theory in German infant care settings, and noted that categories of attachment carry negative moral valuations and are insensitive to cultural differences.

CHAPTER 1

1. See D'Amato, 1993.
2. Spindler, 1959 [1963], p. 148. For example, this theme was treated by Apple & Weiss, 1983; Henry, 1963; Kimball, 1963; Klein, 1972; Lee, 1955; Lewis, 1978; Rosenfeld, 1971, Siegel, 1955.
3. As Harry Wolcott writes:

Schools provide access for learning about American society and for identifying some of the paradoxes that inevitably occur between real and ideal values in specific cultural settings. . . . Central as this idea of a selective and sometimes goal-defeating process of cultural transmission is to understanding either American society or American public education, few writers have described and analyzed elements of it from an anthropological perspective. (Wolcott, 1971, p. 113)

4. Leacock, 1976, p. 240.
5. Jules Henry (1963; 1973), Eleanor Leacock (1971), Dorothy Lee (1955; 1976), Margaret Mead (1951), Hortense Powdermaker (1939), George Spindler (1955), and Gene Weltfish (1965), among others, used their anthropological insights to address what they considered to be weaknesses in contemporary education and society.
6. Kimball, 1963, p. 280.
7. Lave, 1993, p. 26.

CHAPTER 2

1. Veena Das, "Life and Words: Violence and the Descent into the Ordinary." The idea of ordinary violence is also used by Nancy Scheper Hughes in her accounts of life in Brazilian shantytowns; it is also related to the ideas of social structural violence in the work of medical anthropologists such as Arthur Kleinmann and Paul Farmer.

CHAPTER 5

1. Eduardo Porter, "Dropping out of college, and paying the price," *New York Times*, June, 25, 2013.

CHAPTER 6

1. See Baker and LeTendre (2005), *National Differences, Global Similarities* (Stanford, CA: Stanford University Press).

CHAPTER 7

1. See Stevenson and Stigler (1994), *The Learning Gap* (New York: Simon & Schuster).

2. Annette Lareau (2003), *Unequal Childhoods: Class, Race, and Family Life* (Berkeley, CA: University of Calfornia, Berkeley). Lareau's research has shown that middle-class parents have a distinct advantage in supporting and positioning their children for success, because the schools draw upon the advantages of social class that middle-class parents are able to bring to the table.

3. See Baker and LeTendre, 2005, p. 76.

4. Baker and LeTendre, 2005, p. 99.

5. Lesson study is a Japanese professional development practice that is becoming a model for teacher researcher groups around the nation. See Lewis, Perry, and Murata (2006); Fernandez (2002).

6. See Tobin, Wu, and Davidson 1989, and Tobin, Hsueh, and Karasawa, 2009.

7. See Kenneth Zeichner and May Klehr, "Teacher Research as Professional Development for P-12 Educators." The five programs reviewed for the Zeichner/Klehr study include the Madison, Wisconsin, Metropolitan School District classroom action research program; Brookline and Boston (Mass.) Learning/Teaching Collaborative inquiry seminars; the Lawrence School teacher study groups, Brookline (Mass.); the Bay Area (Calif.) professional development consortium teacher action research project; and schoolwide action research in Georgia and Ames, Iowa.

8. This is beautifully documented in the film *Precious Knowledge*, about the efforts of students and teachers in an Arizona public school to keep their ethnic studies program running in the face of concerted political efforts to shut it down.

REFERENCES

Apple, M., and Weis, L. eds. 1983. *Ideology and Practice in Schooling*. Philadelphia: Temple University Press.

Baker, David P., and Gerald K. LeTendre. 2005. *National Differences, Global Similarities: World Culture and the Future of Schooling*. Stanford, CA: Stanford University.

D'Amato, John. 1993. Resistance and Compliance in Minority Classrooms. In E. Jacob and C. Jordan, eds. *Minority Education: Anthropological Perspectives*. Norwood, NJ: Ablex.

Das, Veena. 2006. *Life and Words: Violence and the Descent into the Ordinary*. Berkeley, CA: University of California.

Diamond, Stanley. 1964. A Revolutionary Discipline. *Current Anthropology* 5(5) (Dec. 1964): 432–7.

Fernandez, Clea. 2002. Learning from Japanese Approaches to Professional Development: The Case of Lesson Study. *Journal of Teacher Education* 53: 393-405.

Geertz, Clifford. 1985. The Uses of Diversity. The Tanner Lectures on Human Values. Delivered at the University of Michigan, November 8, 1985.

Henry, J. 1963. *Culture against Man*. New York: Random House.

Henry, J. 1973. *On Sham, Vulnerability, and Other Forms of Self-Destruction*. London: Penguin.

Kimball, S. T. 1963. Cultural Influences Shaping the Role of the Child. In G. D. Spindler, ed. *Education and Culture: Anthropological Approaches*. New York: Harcourt, 268–83.

Lareau, Annette. 2003. *Unequal Childhoods: Class, Race, and Family Life.* Berkeley, CA: Brace College.

Lave, Jean. 1993. The Practice of Learning. In S. Chaiklin and J. Lave, eds. *Understanding Practice: Perspectives on Activity and Context.* New York: Cambridge University, 3–32.

Leacock, Eleanor B. 1976. Education in Africa: Myths of "Modernization." In C. J. Calhoun and A. J. Ianni, ed. *The Anthropological Study of Education.* Chicago: Aldine, 139–250.

Leavitt, Robin. 1994. *Power and Emotion in Infant-Toddler Day Care.* Albany, NY: SUNY press.

Lee, Dorothy. 1955. Discrepancies in the Teaching of American Culture. In G. D. Spindler, ed. *Education and Anthropology.* Stanford, CA: Stanford University, 163–76.

Lee, Dorothy. 1976. *Valuing the Self: What We Can Learn from Other Cultures.* Prospect Heights, IL: Waveland Press.

LeVine, Robert A., and Karin Norman. 2001. The Infant's Acquisition of Culture: Early Attachment Reexamined in Anthropological Perspective. In C. Moore and H. Mathews, eds. *The Psychology of Cultural Experience.* New York: Cambridge University.

Lewis, Catherine, Rebecca Perry, and Aki Murata. 2006. How Should Research Contribute to Instructional Improvement? The Case of Lesson Study. *Educational Researcher* 35(3): 3–14.

Mead, Margaret. 1951. *The School in American Culture.* Cambridge, MA: Harvard University.

Polakow, Valerie. 1992. *The Erosion of Childhood.* Chicago: University of Chicago Press.

Porter, Eduardo. 2013. "Dropping Out of College, and Paying the Price." *New York Times*, June 25.

Powdermaker, Hortense. (1939 [1993]). *After Freedom: A Cultural Study in the Deep South.* New York: Viking. [Reprint, Madison: University of Wisconsin.]

Rosenfeld, Gerry. 1971. *"Shut Those Thick Lips!" A Study of Slum School Failure.* New York: Holt, Rinehart, and Winston.

Siegel, Bernard. 1955. Models for the Analysis of the Educative Process in American Communitites. In G. D. Spindler, ed. *Education and Anthropology.* Stanford, CA: Stanford University, 38–49.

Spindler, G. D. ([1959] 1963). The Transmission of American Culture. In G. D. Spindler, ed. *Education and Culture: Anthropological Approaches.* New York: Holt, Rinehart, and Winston, 148–72.

Stevenson, Harold W., and James W. Stigler. 1994. *The Learning Gap: How Our Schools Are Failing and What We Can Learn from Japanese and Chinese Education.* New York: Simon & Schuster.

Tobin, Joseph, David Wu, and Dana Davidson. 1989. Preschool in Three Cultures. New Haven, CT: Yale University.

Tobin, Joseph, Yeh Hsueh, and Mayumi Karasawa. 2009. Preschool in Three Cultures Revisited. Chicago: University of Chicago.

Tyack, David, and Cuban, Larry. 1997. *Tinkering Toward Utopia: A Century of Public School Reform.* Cambridge, MA: Harvard University.

Valenzuela, Angela. 1999. Subtractive Schooling: U.S.-Mexican Youth and the Politics of Caring. Buffalo, NY: State University of New York.

Weltfish, Gene. 1965. *The Lost Universe.* New York: Basic Books.

Wolcott, H. 1971. Handle with Care: Necessary Precautions in the Anthropology of Schools. In M. L. Wax, S. Diamond, and F. O. Gearing, eds. *Anthropological Perspectives on Education.* New York: Basic Books, 98–117.

Zeichner, Kenneth, and May Klehr. 1999. "Teacher Research as Professional Development for P-12 Educators." Washington, D.C.: National Partnership for Excellence and Accountability in Teaching, Office of Educational Research and Improvement.

ABOUT THE AUTHOR

Diane M. Hoffman is an associate professor of social foundations of education at the Curry School of Education, University of Virginia. She earned her PhD in education from Stanford University, and specializes in the anthropology of education and international comparative education. Her research considers the cultural dimensions of education very broadly, with a special focus on how education reflects and shapes identity in diverse contexts. She has a special interest in multiculturalism, in globalization, and in cultural ideologies surrounding parenting and childhood. Her anthropological fieldwork has focused on Iranian immigrants in U.S. schools, Korean immigrants in Japan, and Haitian youth and children in pre- and post-earthquake Haiti.